NIYI BORIRE
CHARLES BALL
MOFOLUWASO ILEVBARE

SAMUEL EKUNDAYO
ESTHER ADEYINKA
TOLU OLIAKU

CHANGING YOU

THE ULTIMATE COMPENDIUM TO BECOMING A BETTER YOU

CHANGING YOU

DEDICATION

To everyone who desires to be the best that they can be in
an ever-changing world.

ACKNOWLEDGEMENTS

We could not have pulled off this kind of project without the invaluable contributions of great minds.

A big thanks to all the co-authors for bringing on their A-game in sharing practical insights on the topics. God bless and honour you for shining the light through the pages of this book for others to see.

To our able editor, Sam Adetiran, thank you for ensuring that all the pieces came together perfectly to produce this masterpiece.

Opeoluwa Adebakin, our skillful designer, thank you for bringing the book to life through the exquisite designs.

TABLE OF CONTENTS

INTRODUCTION

Why have we chosen the title, **'Changing You'** for this book? It is quite simple. It is because you need to change. Yes, you. 'Change to what?' you may ask. Change to a better you. 'But I am not doing bad,' you may want to argue. Yes, you are right about that. However, you can be better than you are right now. Your present you is certainly not the best you yet. For as long as we are in the world, there is always room for improvement. You can be a better father. You can be a better mother. You can be a better husband. You can be a better wife. You can be a better boss. You can be a better employee. The list goes on. In short, the world can be better because you are consciously getting better.

Change, as they say, is the only constant in life. Everything around us is constantly changing; weather, climate, economy, policies, politics, fashion, etc. Maybe another word for the world would be change. Nothing stays the same. Even when we are not changing actively, change is still happening to us. So, change has come to stay and we must be comfortable with that. Many times, we are demanding for a change. A change in government, a change in salary, a change in our spouses, a change in our children, and so on and we forget to demand the change from the most important person - ourselves. Is that not interesting? That we can easily demand for change from every other thing or person around us except ourselves. We want things and people around us to get better so that the quality of our lives can get better, but we forget that to truly experience that better life, it must start with us.

This book has been written to help put the spotlight of change on you. Yes, you. Not on your spouse, neighbour, government, employer, etc. but you. You are the most important factor in this equation of change and if the world would become a better place for us all, then it must start with you. It is time to hold yourself accountable to higher standards of change. While it is easy to spot the speck in the other person's eyes, it is time to pay attention to the log in your eyes. Enough of highlighting how people can change or where they need to change, it is time to focus on you. It is time to take the lead in personal transformation which will ultimately lead to the national and global transformation that we so desire. If we all focus on ourselves like we should, demanding change for the better continually, our world will naturally become better. Better individuals produce better societies. It is that simple.

What we have done in this book is to point your attention to six major areas of your life that require change: The creative you, the spiritual you, the emotional you, the financial you, the physical you, and the social you. You get to understand yourself more in these six areas, and then you get the relevant information and tools that can help you become a better person in these areas of your life. More interesting is how everything is tied up by exposing you to the neuroscience of change that explains the practicality and predictability of change, thereby putting in your hands a toolkit for a lifetime of transformational change. We cannot wait to hear about your testimonies of change as you devour and apply the principles of long lasting change captured in this compendium. Enjoy your reading.

CHAPTER 1

CHANGING THE CREATIVE YOU

By Samuel Ekundayo

ARE YOU CREATIVE?

Have you ever been asked that question? You may well have been posed the question, either by a curious friend or a potential employer wishing to know more about your problem-solving skills or how talented you are. A friend once asked me the same question, and I found myself bemused and struggled to answer as I had not given much thought to the 'creative' label before then. While I am multi-talented, I have never referred to or labelled myself a creative. It is a question that, though often unintended, tends to classify some people as creative and others as non-creative. It is easy to be confronted with such a question and – perhaps out of humility or moderation, and not wanting to blow your own trumpet – immediately respond, '*No, I am not creative*' or '*I would not quite call myself creative.*' The truth is, this classification may exist in people's minds and our society, but it is a fallacy!

You were created and wired to be creative. Your very essence

1

is full of creativity. This is what separates the human species from animals. While animals generally rely on their instincts to connect to their surroundings and survive, humans rely on the ability to think and rationalise to understand, adapt to our environment, and creatively advance our world. The human mind is the most powerful and creative force in nature. All human developments are largely engineered by the creative power of the mind to generate insights, focus in-depth, and solve uncommon problems. From early humans whose primary goal was surviving in their environment to modern humans whose goal is to advance the world technologically, our creativity has been the source of our growth and development for millions of years. This is how we are wired.

Human potential is one of the only infinite resources we have in the world. Most everything else is finite, but the human mind is the ultimate superpower — there is no limit to our creativity, imagination, determination, or ability to think, reason, or learn. — Jim Kwik

You are creative. You don't need to have attended the best schools in the world to tap into your creative power. You don't need extra-terrestrial powers to be creative. You don't need to understand magic or illusion to be creative. You are creative. You carry the nature of your Creator and part of that nature is creativity. The very first thing we know about God is the fact that He created the heavens and the earth. The first sentence in the Bible that introduces us to God mentions His creative powers. It reads thus, '*In the beginning, God created the heavens and the earth*'. It is as if God wants to show us that an undeniable part of His essence is creativity. It doesn't end there; as everything that followed that statement had to do with Him creating various other things from light to day, to fishes, to plants, and so on. All of the creation displays the amazing creativity of God. David captured this succinctly in the book of Psalms when he said, '*The heavens proclaim the glory of God. The skies display his craftsmanship. Day after day they continue to speak; night after night they make him known. They speak without a sound or word; their voice is never heard. Yet their message has gone throughout the earth, and their words to all the world*'

THE BIOLOGICAL FORCE OF CREATIVITY

One of God's creations that not only displays his creativity but embodies its essence is the human species. If we briefly look at how man was created, we will see the intentionality God put into creating him to carry His creative nature. Two

> *You are creative. You don't need to have attended the best schools in the world to tap into your creative power. You don't need extra-terrestrial powers to be creative. You don't need to understand magic or illusion to be creative.*

powerful biological traits God gave to man that complement his thinking faculty are, the visual and the social. Visually, humans cannot just look but see differently than animals do. We see things and form perspectives that are based on our mind's interpretation of what we see. We can leverage our imaginations to construct and reconstruct the things we see and the things we do not see. On the other hand, we are also social creatures, and in working together, we become an even more powerful force of creativity. These two traits have mothered most of the human developments we have seen to date. If you like, you call them the force of vision and relationships.

This brings to mind what happened at the tower of Babel, where these two powerful traits brought about one of the greatest feats in human history. Millions of years ago, all the people of the world spoke the same language and they were united. One day, they all decided to build a tower that would reach the sky. They envisioned it and because they were united, they were a force to reckon with and their vision was limitless. I love the way God puts it, 'The people are united, and they all speak the same language. After this, nothing they set out to do will be impossible for them.' To stop them, their united front, which was such a powerful force, had to be attacked. God saw beyond what they were trying to do at that point, He was more interested in the power of their vision and unitedness, hence why he said, '*After this, nothing they set out to do will be impossible for them.*' It was not even about that vision but the vision after that and the next, should they continue to be united. Simply put, creativity comes alive when there is a vision, and the people are united. They will just keep creating one thing after the other and doing the impossible together.

THE WORLD NEEDS YOUR CREATIVITY

The world, as it is, is full of problems and crises. From individual lives to family units, from corporate organisations to governmental representation of states worldwide, our world is calling for creative minds who can solve the problems we face. From intangible problems such as mental health disorders, identity crises, and lack of purpose to tangible ones like global warming, and terrorism, the world is desperate for men and women who would tap into their creative powers to save us and restore hope to humanity. Make no mistake thinking these problems began a few decades ago. No! They have always been since the foundation of the world when Adam and Eve made the capital wrong choice. Thousands and possibly millions of years later, people are still making choices that continue to plunder the world further down the bottomless pit of problems and crises.

History makers are people who have found their creative power and have tapped into it to deliver plausible solutions in our world to add value to lives and make our world a better place. You cannot afford to live your term here on earth without tapping into your creative power. Ever since God rested after creation, He has passed the baton to us human beings to follow in His footsteps by making the world a beautiful place. This is why God created trees, but He did not create houses or buildings. He created cotton plants but did not create clothes or fabrics. He created fruits but human beings made juice and wine. We have the authority to create whatever we wish to see in our world. We have the power, and dominion to envision things and bring them into reality. For centuries, throughout all revolutions that exist on earth, we have seen the creative power of human beings lead our developments. The names of ordinary men are imprinted in our history books because they tapped into their creative power to deliver extraordinary solutions that changed the course of history. The good news is that history is not done. We are still writing it. Our generation holds the pen, and it is our duty to tap into our creative power, as ordinary men, and women to do the extraordinary.

THE SOURCE OF CREATIVITY

Creativity is a feat that is not attributed to other created beings except human beings. Only human beings have the power to change the course of the world's history as we know it. We have talked about the power of the human mind, but there is a source deeper than the human mind. The human mind is only a fragment of a higher power. Permit me to take you back to when God created man. The Bible says, *'Then the Lord God formed man from the dust of the ground. He breathed the breath of life into the man's nostrils, and the man became a living person.'* This is the account of man's formation, and we see the secret sauce or ingredient uncommon to other creations that made man such a creative being. The man was the only creature that had the unique privilege of sharing God's breath. While there are other living organisms on earth, only man carries this peculiarity. That breath gave man a spirit and a soul. Other organisms have bodies and souls, only humans have a spirit. No, this is not a religious thing. Every human being has a spirit, which is our connection to the spirit realm. You may call it a gift from God, but it is what makes our creativity to be out of this world. We are able to see things beyond our physical realm and bring them to our realm.

In the scripture earlier stated, the word transliterated as 'breath' is the Hebrew word *nesha ma h* which means divine inspiration or intellect. God's breath gave us a part of His spirit and soul, which divinely inspires His creative nature in us. This is why human beings are capable of doing the extraordinary because we are carriers of God's inspiration. We are able to create things out of nothing! Job caught the revelation of this a few times but perhaps the most profound statement he made about it was, '*But there is a spirit within people, the breath of the Almighty within them, that makes them intelligent.*' The source of our creativity is the breath of God on our inside. Later, I will expand more on how to leverage that breath as your key creative power.

HOW TO HARNESS YOUR CREATIVE POWER

We have come to understand the source of your creative power, and registered the fact that despite the controversial definitions and description of who a creative is in our world, you are a creative! In this section, I want to show you how to tap into your creative power to produce a positive change in our world and make the world a better place.

Discover Your Life's Work

As powerful as we are as human beings, we are finite. We are finite in our calling and life's purpose. By that, I mean, we are not called to do everything. You are most creative in the area of your life's work. Permit me to say it like this, your superpower is best expressed in your life's calling. Outside of your life's calling, you would never see your superpower. In your life's work, you are like a round peg in a round hole. You fit, and because you do, you are able to make things happen that would not ordinarily happen. People who have changed the course of history in our world have done it within the confines of their life's calling and that made them live fulfilled lives. So, I believe, the seat or throne of your creative power is in your life's work.

In order to fulfil your life's work, you have been given some extraordinary

" *He has given us abilities to do certain things so well so as to fulfil our life's calling here on earth.*

abilities that we often call gifts or talents. Your gift is that ability you have to do something so well like you have been divinely empowered to do it. I like how the Bible puts it, '*In his grace, God has given us different gifts for doing certain things well. So if God has given you the ability to prophesy, speak out with as much faith as God has given you. If your gift is serving others, serve them well. If you are a teacher, teach well. If your gift is to encourage others, be encouraging. If it is giving, give generously. If God has given you leadership ability, take the responsibility seriously. And if you have a gift for showing kindness to others, do it gladly.*' In God's generosity, and through His grace, He has given us abilities to do certain things so well so as to fulfil our life's calling here on earth. The Apostle Paul admonishes that we should use our gifts to serve others well. Whilst the list of gifts in the scripture is quite spiritual, God has also given us gifts that are not mentioned and that are common in our world today including sports, engineering, coding and programming, horticulture, etc.

I love Howard Gardner's theory of intelligence where he espoused nine types of intelligence beyond the IQ test scores that often make us categorise some people as unintelligent. His work reveals that all men are intelligent and IQ test scores are very limited in testing human intelligence. He first proposed his theory in his 1983 book, *Frames of Mind*, where he outlined several unique types of intellectual competencies that humans have (see the infographic below):

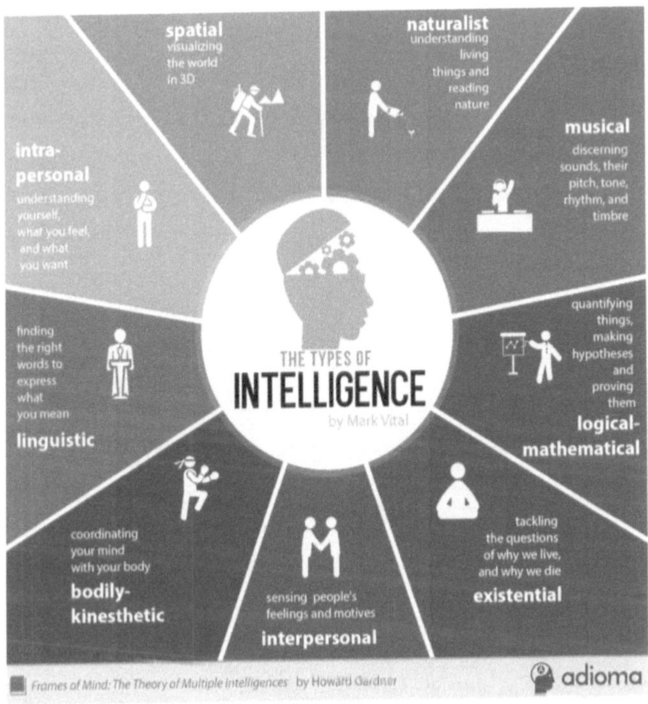

Source: https://blog.adioma.com/9-types-of-intelligence-infographic/

When you look at the nine types of intelligence, you will most likely find you. Your intelligence is your gift and the creativity that flows out of your gift is your gift to the world. For instance, I have three core gifts: Linguistic, existential, and interpersonal. In my work as a speaker and coach, I have used these gifts to help many people find answers to life's tough questions and navigate their quest for purpose discovery and clarity. I have created several courses, programmes, seminars, and conferences centered around my gifts. I am blossoming in my creativity because I have found where I fit. You too can find where you fit so you can blossom in your creativity.

I should say that I do not mean that you are not also creative outside your life's work. You are. You can be a creative mum or dad, a creative professional in your workplace. Other areas I will be discussing will relay how you can harness your creative power whether you are functioning within or outside your life's work.

Leverage the Power of Your Imagination

Einstein said, '*Imagination is more powerful than knowledge.*' I think he is right because knowledge is what is, but imagination is what is not but can be. Imagination is the ability to create a mental picture of things we cannot discern through our five senses. Imagination gives us the ability to think in pictures. If I asked you to close your eyes and try to imagine the next 10 years of your life, what would you see? I could give it more context by asking you to imagine what you are wearing, who you are with, the house you are living in, and the kind of car you are driving with your spouse and kids. The more you imagine these things, the more you keep smiling. You would go on creating what does not yet exist in reality but as you do this, you start to experience some emotions because your mind cannot tell the difference between what you are imagining and what is real. This is why imagination works!

I once read about Michelangelo, the renowned sculptor famous for the Sistine Chapel ceiling, and David's Statue in Rome. The article said that Michelangelo would spend a lot of time staring at a piece of wood just imagining what he would create with it. He was using the power of his imagination to create what he wanted to create in his mind first before chiselling it out on the wood. Most artists do this very well. Like an artist, you can harness your creativity by leveraging the power of your imagination every day! Create the things you would

like to see in your life, in your profession, family, or business using your imagination. When you're done imagining, write them down, and go to work on them. Every great thing you see today started in someone's mind.

I had the opportunity to visit the New Zealand parliament some time ago. The building is popularly referred to as the Beehive. It is the executive wing of the New Zealand parliament building where the Prime minister and the cabinet ministers have their offices and where they meet. It is so-called because it is shaped like a traditional beehive known as a skep. We were told the story of how the architect, Sir Basil Spence, had visited Wellington, the capital city of New Zealand in 1964. While having a meal with the Prime Minister (Keith Holyoake) at the time, armed with only a napkin and pencil, he sketched the concept of the Beehive after successfully convincing the Prime Minister to go for a modern building. History has it that it was received with mixed feelings, but eventually, it was carried out. Decades later, what started as a concept in an architect's mind now sits on an expanse of land as a cynosure for millions of travellers and tourists.

Your intelligence is your gift and the creativity that flows out of your gift is your gift to the world.

Like the Beehive, every great thing that has ever been done in history began as a concept, a picture, or an image in someone's mind, but they did not stop there. They got their hands dirty and they eventually brought their imagination to reality. This is why we celebrate them. I love how Aristotle defined perception, imagination, and intellect. I think it is really interesting. He said, '*Perception is a power of the body, intellect is a power of the mind, and imagination is a power of the spirit.*' I think I agree with Aristotle. Imagination is spiritual. It is a spiritual power that is capable of making the unseen visible.

Create Thinking Time

Creativity begins in the human mind and a major work of the mind is thinking. To harness the power of your thoughts, you have to be intentional about it. In other words, you have to make time to think creatively. We live in a world full of distractions and it is very easy to be so distracted that you won't find the time to think unless you are intentional about it. This is why the majority of people find it hard to be creative and productive. They wake up in the morning and by the time it is night, they wonder where the time has gone, as they have nothing to show. One of the keys to harnessing your creative power is ensuring no day goes by without intentionally making time to think.

It will not happen automatically, so you would need to schedule it in your calendar. I am very intentional about this, such that at 10 p.m. every day, I take a few minutes to sit at my office desk at home just to think. I like to think a lot on paper so, often, I would draw mind maps about a specific thing or project I am working on. I found this to be an effective way of brain-dumping my ideas on paper. I have it on my calendar too every day. Once it is fifteen minutes to 10, I get a reminder on my phone about it, and I start mentally wrapping up whatever I was doing around that time. I have found that because it is scheduled on my calendar, it is more like I have given myself the chance to follow through with it. I treat it like I would any other appointment on my calendar and show up on my desk with my pen and paper.

Another thing I do is to shun every distraction at the time. My greatest distraction is my phone. The notifications from message apps and social media can be so distracting for me. Knowing this about myself, I have intentionally put my phone on 'Do Not Disturb' from 10 p.m. every night. I must confess, it takes a while to get into this focused mode. This is why I start by reading my bible and whatever book I'm reading on the day, and just switch into thinking when my focus is at its optimum. Most of my creative ideas have come from this practice.

I have found it helps not to rush the process. The reason many people do not derive much from their thinking time is they are often rushing it. Also, it is not every thinking time that would lead to a solution or

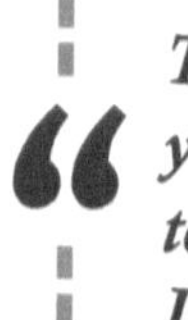

To harness the power of your thoughts, you have to be intentional about it. In other words, you have to make time to think creatively.

decision about whatever you have made time to think about but do not be discouraged. All possible alternatives or mappings you have done are still feathers to your cap. Come back the next day. This is why it is so important to make a habit of it. I do not encourage having your thinking time set for less than thirty minutes. Anything shorter would seem like a rush and may be hard to get your focus optimal enough for creativity. Some people suggest setting a timer, but I have never done this so I cannot advise on its effectiveness.

Put Your Brain in a Reward State

Neurologists and psychologists have told us that our brain is often scanning for threats. As a result, by default, our brains are usually in threat mode most of the time. Unfortunately, this is the worst state for our brains to generate insights - epochal revelations and realisations — that move our lives forward. Insights are the deeply rewarding moments when we go from, '*I do not know what to do*' or '*I cannot seem to figure this out*' to '*Aha! I have found a solution*' or '*Aha! I got it.*' These moments are critical for our creativity. We are told that our brain generates more insights when it is in a reward or rest state. In a rest or reward state, our brain is more motivated. It takes a lot of intentionality to put your brain in a reward or rest state.

Be intentional about safeguarding your mind such that you are consistently in a reward state. There are elements that the brain perceives directly as rewards, e.g. food, sleep, water (shower or regularly drinking water), air, shelter, money, sex, etc. However, there are some less obvious rewards you have to ensure you put around your life including:

Predictability – less disruption to your routine.

Social acceptance – being around people who celebrate you, not just tolerate you. Opportunities for advancement – be in environments or with people who encourage you to grow and develop.

Learning – an environment where you are sharpening your skills or gaining mastery, etc.

You have to be intentional to create an environment that nurtures your creative power.

Mind Your Relationships

Jim Rohn said that you are an average of the five people you spend the most time with. This means if you want to nurture your creative power, you must be around people who are nurturing theirs. If you surround yourself with creative people, you will eventually develop your creative potential. Your ideas are the seeds of your creativity. You must put yourself in environments where generating ideas is encouraged and those ideas are supported. It was Charlie Brower who said that a new idea is delicate. It can be killed by a sneer or a yawn; it can be stabbed to death by a quip and worried to death by a frown on the right man's brow. Negative environments kill great ideas. A creative environment, on the other hand, is like a greenhouse where ideas are seeded, then sprout and thrive.

Environments determine the conversations that fill your life. The issue with the wrong environment is the kind of conversations that take place in that environment. You would consistently listen to conversations that kill or drown your creativity and ideas. Phrases that are common to such environments are, 'Who do you think you are to think like that?', 'That is not logical?', 'Your idea is not practical', 'Your idea is not logical', 'It has never been done', 'It is impossible', 'Do not be foolish to think you can do that here', 'It will be too hard to do', 'We do not have the time', 'We do not have the money or resources', 'This sort of idea is not for people like us.'

You need to be intentional about the relationships you keep and the conversations you are consistently participating in. I once heard Lisa Nichol share her story. She grew up in an environment where most of the women struggled to put food on their table and dated men who were gang members or ended up in prison. One day, she realised she had become one of those women. She had a son whose father was in prison and was struggling to eat. That day, something rose within her, and she was determined to change the narrative. She packed her things, got in her car with her son, and headed to New York to attend a seminar. She got to the seminar and everything they were saying seemed like a foreign language to her, but she stayed. They were talking about raising funds, traveling the world, starting companies, and talking to investors. Those kinds of things were strange to her. No one, where she was coming from, ever said those things. That was the first day of the rest of her life. She changed her environment, changed her conversations, and everything changed. Within a few years, she was a bestselling author and became a millionaire, travelling the world, sharing her story, and inspiring other women.

Your creativity will never blossom in the wrong environment. A rose in the wrong environment would look like a weed. For instance, roses need to be where they would receive six to eight hours of sunlight daily. That is where they would bloom to their fullest potential. Many people are roses, but they are in dark rooms. Their creative potential would never see the light of day. The right environment for you to bloom would encourage creativity. You must situate yourself in rooms and places where innovation and good thinking are encouraged and rewarded. You must put yourself where everyone is comfortable to create things. The right environment for you would encourage you to try and fail. You should not be in an environment where you are not free to experiment. You must be willing to try several times until you succeed. The right environment for you would encourage you to dream and dream big. You must be willing to dare yourself to create big things.

The people who would help you harness your creative potential would be people who are also creating things and have made creativity a priority. They are regularly taking time

Your creativity will never blossom in the wrong environment. A rose in the wrong environment would look like a weed.

to think and do big things. My friends are people like this. People who would help you harness your creativity must be people who inspire you. These people energise you. They spark a surge in your creativity. They are comfortable with their uniqueness and celebrate your uniqueness too. They lift you and never put you down. Even when they offer feedback, the goal is to amplify your creativity, not to dampen it.

Invest In Knowledge

I once heard the story of a dentist who went to a conference outside of his hometown. At the conference, he learnt about a new dental implant technique. While he had his clinic and had been practicing for years in his hometown, it was the first time he'd attended a conference of such stature. He brought the technique back to his hometown. To his surprise, beyond his hometown to neighbouring towns and cities, most dentists were yet to hear about this new technique. He began helping many patients and his business skyrocketed. Not only that, he began training other dentists around and made a lot of money doing so. All he did was invest in knowledge.

Creativity is not just about generating new ideas; you can leverage the ideas of others to create solutions you would be rewarded for. However, you must position yourself to hear about them. I often challenge my students, mentees, and coaching clients to shop around for their greatness. By this I mean, be intentional about paying for the right courses and programmes that will help you generate new insights for your life. In any area of your life where you are struggling, someone is thriving. You just need to hear about what they are doing to thrive so you can learn too.

You must be intentional about reading books. Recently, I was reading a book written in the 1990s about real estate and I found out that the principles of investing in real estate remain the same after many years. *Creativity is not just about generating new ideas; you can leverage the ideas of others to create solutions you would be rewarded for.* Only the methods have changed a bit, but the principles remain the same. Putting to practice what I learnt from the book has helped my wife and me in our real estate investment. I pay thousands of dollars to join a community of speakers and coaches who engage in the conversations that help me become a better speaker and coach. I have never regretted the decision of those investments. I will gladly do more because that is how I got to where I am and that is how I will get to the place of my vision. One such community hosts a monthly hangout where experts come to share their knowledge of the industry. From those hangouts, I hear about new practices, methods, strategies, systems, software, and structures I need to put in place for my business. This is how I break frontiers and expand my horizons.

PUTTING IT ALL TOGETHER

The seat of your creativity is your mind. It is the powerhouse for generating ideas that move your life forward and advance your vision. You must be intentional with the business of your mind to develop your creative potential. God made you special and unique. He gave you a spirit, a soul, and a body. Your spirit and soul are the seat of your creativity. You are spiritual and have spiritual powers which include your imagination – use them! Be intentional about your focus and watch the environment you put yourself in. You are creative and you should stop at nothing to live up to that identity. I believe in you.

CHAPTER 2

CHANGING THE SPIRITUAL YOU

By Niyi Borire

The football world received the shock of their lives when the underdog club, Leicester City Football Club, defied the odds by the bookmarkers (5000-1) to win the prestigious Premier League title of the 2015-2016 campaign. It was baffling, to say the least, that a club that had narrowly escaped relegation the season prior would be crowned the champions of England. It is quite understandable when the big boys do their thing. They are known for that - doing the big things. But it is a different feeling when the underdogs do big things. That was the story of Leicester. They simply did the unthinkable. No one gave them the chance.

This was how Tom Adams summarised it; 'Some incredible stories have been written in football's long history, but nothing quite like this. Leicester's title win was the story of a manager who used pizza as a motivational tool; players who won by not having the ball; a team that was supposed to be relegated but won the league; a club which had no right to elbow its way past the super clubs in an era when finances govern everything. It was the story of a group of men prevailing against all odds, trusting in their own quality and spirit, being ignored and disrespected by their peers, until it was too late, and finally achieving something thought impossible. The power of belief and hard work.'

What makes an underdog team become the champions? What makes a struggling team suddenly become the winning team? What makes people who were not given a chance steal the show? What makes people do the impossible; go against the odds, weather the storms, break the limits, and so on? From where comes willpower, resilience, courage, devotion, creativity, endurance, etc.? What part of man transcends physical and mental limitations to achieve outstanding results? What makes people walk through adversity and come out strong on the other side? Surely, there is a part of man that is unseen but powerful enough to influence what can be seen. This is the part of man that makes him powerful, achieving extraordinary things even while many times looking so ordinary. Certainly, there is more to a man than what can be seen with eyes. Would it be safe to say that man, though natural, can be supernatural?

You may not be a movie lover but indulge me a little. You probably must have heard about the Marvel superheroes series. Then names such as Superman, Spiderman, Batman, Wonder Woman, Captain America, Iron Man, Thor, Black Panther, etc. should not be so strange to you. These are characters who have gotten viewers (both children and adults) glued to their TV screens or thronging to the cinemas over the years. From the comics to the movies, these characters are so intriguing to watch that they always leave their viewers wanting more.

The constant theme in the series is a showcasing of the supernatural or the fact that there are superhumans (who though look natural or

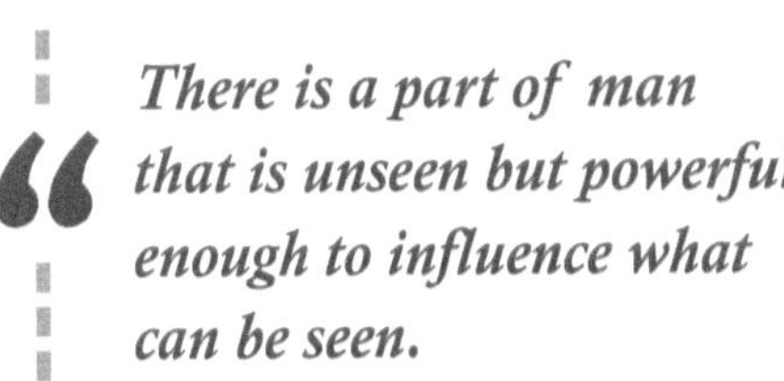

normal) possess abilities that are not common, produce feats that are outrageous, and you cannot but fall in love with the roles that they play. The viewers are able to connect and would keep watching because there is a part in every man that is supernatural (spiritual) which can be ignited by a supernatural entity or act.

When people watch superhero movies one or more of the following happens. The acronym SUPERHERO has been used for ease of connection and remembrance:

- **S**parks creativity: The creativity displayed in these movies would naturally cause a spark in the creativities of the viewers. Their imaginations are set loose and they are able to see possibilities.

- **U**nsettles passivity: Superheroes are always called upon to act because of dire situations that often require their interventions. This would unsettle passivity in anyone as they begin to see the need to act or take responsibility for their own lives or those of others around them.

· **P**ropels you to achieve something: Watching superheroes do their thing propels you to want to achieve something too. It propels you to want to make a difference.

· **E**ncourages Transformation: One of the most interesting things about superhero movies is how the characters transform from seemingly normal human beings into superhumans when their help is needed.

· **R**edirects you to your inner self to draw strength: Even when faced with seemingly insurmountable obstacles, they always turn to their inner self to draw the strength that they need to overcome. So, viewers are inspired to pay attention to their inner selves and draw strength per time.

· **H**elps to bond with others: Superheroes are easy to fall in love with by the people who receive their help. And the superheroes themselves often go all out to help because they feel a connection with the people. It is safe to say that superheroes exist because of the people. So, the value for lives and the need to be a part of other people's lives are heightened.

- **E**ngenders problem-solving skills: Superheroes are problem solvers. They constantly seek ways to solve the problems they encounter, thereby bringing out the problem-solving skills in their viewers.

- **R**estores hope: Superheroes are almost synonymous with hope. They bring hope to the people they serve or help and this in turn inspires hope in the people who watch them; a belief that things will be better or they can do better themselves.

- **O**pens up to possibilities: One thing that is common with superheroes is endless possibilities. They just keep showing that it can be done and get it done, inspiring their viewers to believe in possibilities.

MAN IS A SPIRIT

Truth be told, every man is more than flesh and blood. There is more to our existence than what can be seen or felt. Some folks actually think life is all about what they can process intellectually. So, once it does not make sense to them, they discard or discredit it. Man, essentially, is a spirit who has a soul and lives in a body. That is why man is described as a tripartite being. And the reason is not farfetched, every creation is a reflection of its source and produces after its kind. Man was created by God, hence looks like God. Then God said, *'Let us make human beings in our image, to be like us. They will reign over the fish in the sea, the birds in the sky, the livestock, all the wild animals on the earth, and the small animals that scurry along the ground.'* Man was created to be like God who is a Spirit. It was when God breathed into man that he became a living being, *'Then the* LORD *God formed a man from the dust of the ground and breathed into his nostrils the breath of life, and the man became a living being.'* This is so profound. It is clear that the essence of every man is the breath of God – the unseen (spiritual) that gives life to the seen (physical). So, a man at his core is spiritual, whether he realises it yet or not. It is the reason why humans can be moved by spiritual or supernatural agencies such as the superhero movies we talked about earlier. A part of them is awakened or being stirred. It is with his spirit that a man relates to the spiritual world and makes him long for spiritual experiences.

COMPOSITION OF THE HUMAN SPIRIT

Just in case you are still wondering how man is a spirit, in this section we will talk about what makes up the human spirit. It is believed that the human spirit is made up of three major parts. In an article by Tom Smith titled, *What Is the Function of Your Spirit?* he explained, with the aid of a diagram, these three major parts of the human spirit:

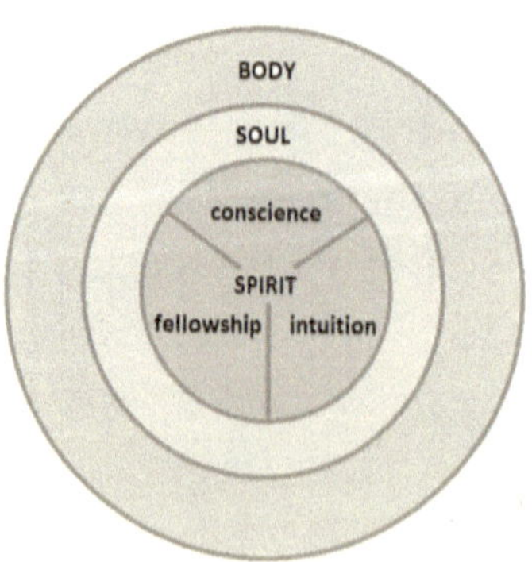

Conscience

You must already be familiar with the word conscience. Wikipedia defines conscience as the ethical or moral sense of right and wrong, chiefly as it affects a person's own behaviour and forms their attitude to their past actions. Meaning that every man's conscience is more like the umpire pre-installed in them to determine what is right or wrong. Therefore, our actions or inactions are determined by our consciences which is a faculty of our spirits.

Fellowship

This is the part of the human spirit that longs for a connection with divinity. Because the

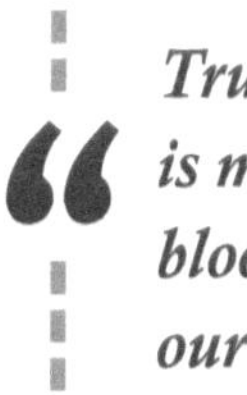

Truth be told, every man is more than flesh and blood. There is more to our existence than what can be seen or felt.

human spirit emanated from God who is in constant fellowship with the Trinity, every man longs for that spiritual fellowship with their source - God. This is why humans tend towards religion. As Greg Laurie said, *'Religion is man's attempt to reach God and Christianity is God's attempt to reach man.'* Men have devised different means to try to fill this vacuum in their spirits that can only be filled by God. That longing for a supernatural connection or fellowship that is characteristic of the human spirit is what makes people go into occultic practices, etc. Man is spiritual and that spirituality will always seek expression. It is left to each individual to go about it the right way and for the right reasons.

God seeks to fellowship with the man He made. 'We proclaim to you what we ourselves have actually seen and heard so that you may have fellowship with us. And our fellowship is with the Father and with his Son, Jesus Christ.' He desires our spiritual worship. "*For God is Spirit, so those who worship him must worship in spirit and in truth.*' No other form of spiritual worship to any other god, deity, or idol will ever satisfy the human spirit. Only fellowship with God's Spirit can fill that hunger.

Intuition

This is a faculty of the human spirit that helps it to 'just know' things. Wikipedia defines it this way:

1. Immediate cognition without the use of conscious rational processes.

2. A perceptive insight gained by the use of this faculty.

This is the reason why you hear people say things such as, 'Something told me to…' or 'I just knew that was going to happen' This is the spirit of a man at work. The spiritual realm is very real and the spirit of a man is very powerful. Our intuitions help us know things supernaturally without conscious thinking. It is a knowing that cannot be explained. Our spirits have been designed to know things about our lives. 'It is only our own spirit within us that knows all about us; in the same way, only God's Spirit knows all about God.'

However, this 'knowing' is still a result of God's workings in our spirits. As the scriptures say, '*But there is a spirit within people, the breath of the Almighty within them, that makes them intelligent.*' We established earlier that the spirit of a man was breathed into him by God. It is this same spirit that makes men spiritually intelligent. Let's take a peep into spiritual intelligence at this point.

SPIRITUAL INTELLIGENCE

'Definitions of spiritual intelligence rely on the concept of spirituality as being distinct from religiosity - existential intelligence.

Danah Zohar defined 12 principles underlying spiritual intelligence:

1. Self-awareness: Knowing what I believe in and value, and what deeply motivates me.

2. Spontaneity: Living in and being responsive to the moment.

3. Being vision- and value-led: Acting from principles and deep beliefs, and living accordingly.

4. Holism: Seeing larger patterns, relationships, and connections; having a sense of belonging.

5. Compassion: Having the quality of "feeling-with" and deep empathy.

6. Celebration of diversity: Valuing other people for their differences, not despite them.

7. Field independence: Standing against the crowd and having one's own convictions.

8. Humility: Having the sense of being a player in a larger drama, of one's true place in the world.

9. Tendency to ask fundamental "Why?" questions: Needing to understand things and get to the bottom of them.

10. Ability to reframe: Standing back from a situation or problem and seeing the bigger picture or wider context.

11. Positive use of adversity: Learning and growing from mistakes, setbacks, and suffering.

12. Sense of vocation: Feeling called upon to serve, to give something back.'

This further corroborates the fact that man is very spiritual and deals with his environment, and world at large, spiritually. Hence, the need to be spiritually aware and inclined.

CHANGING THE SPIRITUAL YOU

In this section, I would love us to consider 12 other expressions of the human spirit that can give you a clue of where you are at and what you need to do to change the spiritual you. The acronym, SPIRITUAL YOU, has been used to describe these expressions:

1.   Sympathy

'[14] Jesus saw the huge crowd as he stepped from the boat, and he had compassion on them and healed their sick. [15] That evening the disciples came to him and said, "This is a remote place, and it's already getting late. Send the crowds away so they can go to the villages and buy food for themselves." [16] But Jesus said, "That isn't necessary—you feed them." [17] "But we have only five loaves of bread and two fish!" they answered. [18] "Bring them here," he said. [19] Then he told the people to sit down on the grass. Jesus took the five loaves and two fish, looked up toward heaven, and blessed them. Then, breaking the loaves into pieces, he gave the bread to the disciples, who distributed it to the people. [20] They all ate as much as they wanted, and afterward, the disciples picked up twelve baskets of leftovers. [21] About 5,000 men were fed that day, in addition to all the women and children!'

Compassion is a gift we give to others by identifying with their situations and taking the initiative to do something about it. From the passage above, Jesus saw people who needed healing and went ahead to heal them. And then went ahead to provide them with food. Our spirits have the capacity to be compassionate towards others, as God's children. 'You must be compassionate, just as your Father is compassionate.' God will not require from us what we do not have the capacity to produce. If He says we should be compassionate, then we have what it takes to be compassionate. However, we must be deliberate about being compassionate.

That is why the Apostle Paul said, 'Therefore, as God's chosen people, holy and dearly loved, clothe yourselves with compassion, kindness, humility, gentleness and patience.' It is one thing to have a cloth, but another thing entirely to put it on. You have sympathy as one chosen by God. It is right there in your spirit. However, you must be deliberate about putting it on and allowing others to be blessed by it.

2.   Purpose

There is a longing for meaning, direction, and fulfilment in every human. It is a deep-seated yearning for relevance. This is purely a spiritual expression which was coded by God from the beginning. Man was created for a purpose as seen in the Book of the Beginnings, *'[26] Then God said, "Let us make human beings in our image, to be like us. They will reign over the fish in the sea, the birds in the sky, the livestock, all the wild animals on the earth, and the small animals that scurry along the ground." [27] So God created human beings in his own image. In the image of God, he created them; male and female he created them. [28] Then God blessed them and said, "Be fruitful and multiply. Fill the earth and govern it. Reign over the fish in the sea, the birds in the sky, and all the animals that scurry along the ground."'*

Every man was created in the image of God for the purpose of God - to be fruitful, multiply, fill the earth, govern it, and reign, in short, have dominion. This is a spiritual mandate with a spiritual blessing. So, purpose in life is purely a spiritual affair. It is spiritual. And only those who are in tune with this spiritual reality can find fulfillment in life. It is the longing of every human spirit to do something or become something. It is how we have been wired.

This is the reason for the questions that everyone needs to ask and answer in their lifetime.

Why am I here on earth?

What am I meant to be contributing?

What do I have to offer?

Where do I need to go?

Who do I need to work with?

Are you aware of your purpose for living? Have you received clarity about your dominion mandate? Where do you need to be fruitful? What are you meant to be multiplying? In what sphere are you supposed to be exerting rulership? What are you meant to be replenishing? Are you fulfilling your purpose? Are you finding fulfillment? What needs to change about this *spiritual you*?

3.   Ingenuity

Look at the world around us and you see different products of man's creativity. Men have constantly pushed the limits of inventions and innovations. There was a time when people never thought man could fly in the air. There was a time when people could never have imagined that man would one day go into space and visit other planets. There was a time when it looked impossible for people to communicate across continents without having to travel. Creativity is a component of the human spirit; evidence that he indeed was created by God who is the Creator of all things. To be creative is to give expression to the *spiritual you*. How much have you explored your creativity? Is the world benefitting from your ingenuity? What solutions are you providing? What ideas are you generating that can positively impact your generation?

### 4.	Resolution

One of the gifts God gave humanity is the ability to make their choices. Every human being has the willpower to do whatever they want to do whenever they want to do it. And this is purely spiritual. So, the measure of your spiritual strength and depth can be seen in the things you decide to do.

'If you have a willing attitude and obey, then you will again eat the good crops of the land.'

How do you approach live decisions? How willing are you to get the best out of life? How have you trained yourself to stay through the cause and push until you get what is rightfully yours? How is your resolve?

### 5.	Imagination

The hopes of the godly result in happiness, but the expectations of the wicked come to nothing. The ability to be expectant (imagine and expect the best) is spiritual. What are your expectations about life? What possibilities are you conjuring? What do you hope to see? What pictures of the future are you seeing? What are you hoping for?

Your imagination is very powerful and God recognises this power of your spirit. There is the story of men who imagined doing something and went all out for it so much that God has this to say about the power of their imagination; *'And the LORD said, Behold, the people is one, and they have all one language; and this they begin to do: and now nothing will be restrained from them, which they have imagined to do.'*

6.   Temerity

'For God has not given us a spirit of fear and timidity, but of power, love, and self-discipline.'

The spirit that God installed in you is not that of timidity or fear but of temerity and boldness. To be fearful and cowardly in life is to act untrue to type. God expects us to approach life with courage regardless of the situations that come against us.

More than ever before, we have come to a time and season of life when we need all the courage we can muster because of the uncertainties and difficulties that stare us in the face. Walking in victory is not for the fainthearted. To take our possessions (the things that are rightfully ours), we must be courageous.

How courageous are you to face obstacles and life challenges? How courageous are you to take on the territories that have been laid in your heart? How courageous are you to stand in your place as an authority in your field of endeavour?

7.　　Understanding

'But it is the spirit in a person, the breath of the Almighty, that gives them understanding.'

The understanding of mysteries is a deeply spiritual affair. There are things that are beyond human reasoning or calculations. We live in a world of mysteries and we need understanding per time to be able to walk in their realities.

'This was because a special spirit was found in this Daniel whom the king called Belteshazzar. He had much learning and understanding to tell the meaning of dreams and secrets and to give answers to problems. Call for Daniel, and he will tell you what this means.' By divine inspiration and alignment with God's Spirit, our spirits can walk in deep realms of understanding that would make us solution providers in our different spheres of existence.

8.　　Adjustability

In different seasons and at different times, we will be exposed to different life situations or circumstances that would demand flexibility or adaptability from us. Rigidity will limit our growth and relevance in life. It is important to be flexible and adaptable. Hence, we need to be free-spirited.

9.　　Lenience

Which faculty helps us to forgive people for their wrongdoings no matter how hurtful? Forgiveness is of the heart or spirit.

'bearing with one another and, if one has a complaint against another, forgiving each other; as the Lord has forgiven you, so you also must forgive.'

Forgiveness is a deeply spiritual exercise and only those who have built the capacity of their spirits would be able to practice forgiveness.

How easily do you forgive others when they offend you? Do you keep records of wrongs done to you? Do you hold grudges when people hurt you? How strong is your spirit to forgive?

10. Youthfulness

'That is why we never give up. Though our bodies are dying, our spirits are being renewed every day.' One beautiful thing about the spirit is renewed strength. Our outward man (physical bodies) may become old or get weaker, but the inward man (the spirit) is continually renewed.

Have you seen seemingly old people who sound so lively and youthful that you wonder where the strength is coming from? They look frail bodily, yet sound so strong. They are people whose spirits are still very lively. Over the years, they have learnt to keep their spirits bubbly.

'The human spirit sustains a sick person, but who can bear a broken spirit?'

Even in sickness, a man can be sustained by his spirit. How youthful are you in your spirit? How strong are you within?

11.   Optimism

'And we know that God causes everything to work together for the good of those who love God and are called according to his purpose for them.'

Optimism is a positive outlook on life. It is the belief that things will turn out well or work out well. Optimistic people are lively people and are an encouragement to be around. Even in the midst of difficulty, they are seeing possibilities.

Their spirits are full of positivity, and no negativity thrives around them. Optimism is a spiritual virtue. How optimistic are you? What is your outlook on life? How do you see difficulties and adversities?

12.   Uprightness

'We are careful to be honorable before the Lord, but we also want everyone else to see that we are honorable.'

God, our Creator, is holy. There is no blemish in Him. He expects us to also conduct our lives to depict uprightness in words and actions.

Uprightness, integrity, or honesty are virtues that emanate from our spirits. How robust is your spirit to accommodate other people's faults and weaknesses?

HOW DO YOU CHANGE THE SPIRITUAL YOU?

We have looked at different expressions of the spiritual you that should help you see where you stand and where you need to improve. That is where your journey of change begins - acknowledging where you are and accepting that something needs to be done to get better. So, the question on your mind now must be, 'How can I change the *spiritual me*?' We will attempt to answer that in this last section of the chapter.

Changing the *spiritual you* simply means the things you need to do to be more in touch with your spiritual (higher) self and ensure that it finds expression as it should. Below are a few tips that can help:

1. Fellowship: Man was created to fellowship with His Maker (as we have seen earlier under the components of the spirit). To be in touch with your spirit and give it its fullest expression, you need to make a habit of being in an atmosphere of fellowship. This can be done through praying, fasting, and reading or studying God's Word for yourself. This could also be achieved in any spiritual gathering of like-minded people that helps you touch God and commune with others.

2. Read and Study: *Give yourself to reading or studying God's Word which is the primary food for your spirit to grow* and also books or materials written by spiritual people who have shared from the wealth of their own experiences.

3. Meditation: *'Reflect on what I am saying, for the Lord will give you insight into all this.'* You must make it a habit to reflect as this opens the door of understanding to you which in turn helps you to maximise your spirit.

4. Serve: Commit yourself to causes higher than you. Be useful. Find a problem you can solve. Put a demand on your inward man. Serve others. Do something that would help others. This is the best way to ultimately find purpose because you will soon find out what makes your heart beat and that thing that you can spend the rest of your life doing. Purpose and relevance in life are found on the path of service.

> *Changing the spiritual you simply means the things you need to do to be more in touch with your spiritual (higher) self and ensure that it finds expression as it should.*

5. Exercise your faith: Faith is the currency of the spirit. 'By faith we understand that the universe was formed at God's command, so that what is seen was not made out of what was visible.' It is by faith that we exercise our spirits. It is by faith that we stretch our spiritual muscles so that we can be creative like God, bringing the seen out of the unseen, and commanding results. Believe God for something greater than you. Trust

God to do something great in and through you. Set your spirit loose!

6. Put your willpower to work: Do not just accept everything thrown at you. Put your power of choice to work. Choose good over bad. Make the tough calls. Choose the right path. Do not settle for less. Take charge and be in charge.

7. Use the power of words: Words are powerful. Words are spirits. Words are building blocks. Use your words wisely and creatively. Speak life, speak abundance, speak healing, speak into existence what you want to see. You are a life-giving spirit indwelt by the Life-Giving Spirit, so speak life all around you.

CHAPTER 3

CHANGING THE EMOTIONAL YOU

By Charles Ball

DO NOT CRY OVER SPILLED MILK!

This is the true story of a mother's struggle with anger, sadness, emotional turbulence, and change. Jane was a single mother of three children. Their father migrated to another country to seek a better life for himself — yes, not for his family — for himself only. Having given birth to the first of the children at around nineteen years old, Jane was young and had not had a fair chance at developing herself and securing a solid foundation for her future and that of her children. She had been anchored in one place by three living, breathing, and eating attachments that needed her as much as she needed support to raise them.

On one particular unforgettable night, Jane's youngest son was gripped by the pangs of hunger that he could express only through uncontrollable wailing. Determined to rescue him from the violent contractions of his stomach which could only be sated by nourishment, Jane found the single source of food that her humble home had to offer, a can with the sticky remains of some condensed milk that stubbornly clung to the bottom as if determined to be thrown out in the container with tomorrow's trash. She poured some water on the milk and swirled it around, hoping to preserve some semblance of the milk's flavour by not overdiluting it. The final act of the preparation was to carefully pour it into a cup being careful not to waste a drop. Jane then instructed her son to sit on the floor, and then she placed the cup in front of him. Finally, satisfaction was in sight, but Jane was not prepared for what happened next.

As the young boy positioned himself to take hold of his drink, one swift movement of his short but powerful leg sent the milk spilling all over the wooden floorboards in front of him. At that moment, he looked to his mother as if for her to explain the impossibility of that fleeting moment that sent them hurling back to their original situation quicker than he had had the satisfaction of escaping it even momentarily. Jane watched as the milk seemed all too determined to disappear hastily into the cracks of the old flooring, and then she had an idea that turned into an instruction. Jane told her son to prostrate as if to pray and lick the milk from the floor, and quickly! The boy obeyed his mother and bent over and with every bit of the suction ability that his small lungs could afford, he slurped, sucked, and licked all that he could until all that remained of his unfortunate dinner accident were the damp, sticky stains of his spilled milk.

If you have ever wondered if anyone has ever cried over spilled milk, witnessing Jane in the deluge of tears and despair would have settled all your doubts. She wept bitterly, not so much for the milk, but for the mistakes of her past, for the debasement of her son who was licking milk from the floor like an animal, for the anger and pain that were rooted in the abandonment that she felt from the man who had left her to eke out a living without a thought of how she would manage all on her own with their children. She

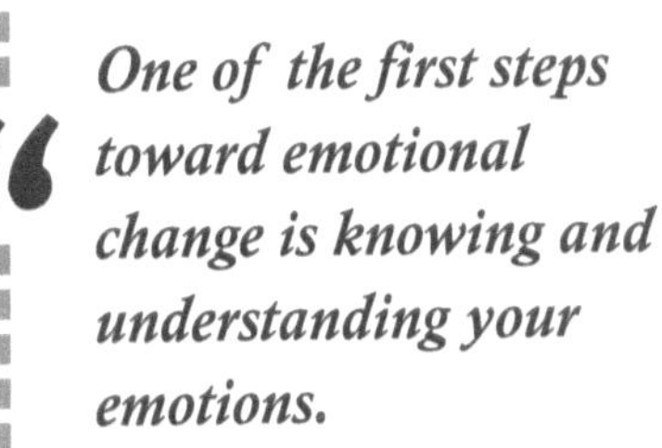

had lost all hope. She was despondent. She felt hopeless, unaccomplished, incapable, and like she had been left to perish in a cauldron of every seething negative emotion her brain could manufacture. She was broken.

After many more tumultuous hardships, including the death of one of her three children, Jane's life finally took a turn for the better. Many years later, she met and married a man who was kind to her and supported her children as though they were his own. However, during a trip abroad one year, the unthinkable happened, she came face to face with the father of her children – more than twenty years after she last saw him. He laughed, stared, and smiled out of genuine excitement to see her. At this point, you might think that she would have gone full grenade mode on the man and blown him to pieces with the most vicious verbal onslaught that she had cautiously curated for many years for such a chance encounter. Nope! Jane greeted him with the most genuine smile and compassionate embrace. She had forgiven him and moved on with her life. Jane harboured nothing in the form of resentment toward him for shirking his paternal duties and leaving her to suffer as she did. She loved him like a friend.

At this point, your eyebrows are probably knitted into tight knots as you wonder how such a thing could be. Maybe you have even already concocted a list of the most abrasive and stinging adjectives that you would have used to whip the man to death if you had been in Jane's position. How dare he come smiling after all he did to her and their kids. If you have experienced such emotions or others close to them, it is an assurance that you are human, and your feelings are valid. Now, take a deep breath, centre yourself again for a moment, and release the rancour from your soul toward this man. After all, you are only reading about the story, Jane lived through it. How did she do it? How did she learn to let it go? How did she crawl out of the shadow of the feelings that had her corralled into a corner, seemingly with no escape? How did she experience emotional change? And if you have been through something similar or any experience that has left you down and out, is there hope for you too? You bet there is! Let us learn a little about emotions and then we will return to Jane's story.

DO I HAVE EMOTIONS?

One of the first steps toward emotional change is knowing and understanding your emotions. Do you remember the last time you cried uncontrollably because you got hungry? How about the last time you threw yourself on the ground and screamed and wailed until you had your way? Well, if you are thinking to yourself, '*Why would I do that? I am not a baby. I am a grown man/woman!*', those infantile behaviours are as innate to normally developing humans as is our ability to naturally learn the language of our environment. We are all born as emotional beings, but like so many of our other traits and individual character possibilities, we are taught to suppress and gag our emotions into submission. Many people fall into the category of those who like to think that they are tough because they don't show their emotions. What's more, they might even try to instruct others in their 'emotionless' ways, even children, especially boys in some cultures, by telling them to stop being so emotional when their feelings start seeping through the cracks of their armour.

> *An emotion can be described simply as a quick bodily or mental reaction to an internal or external event or situation.*

However, what we might not know is that we all have emotions whether we show them or not. And guess what? They play a big role in our daily decisions, our interactions with strangers, and especially the people who are close to us. For example, have you ever wondered why we are so much more likely to hurt the people who are close to us? They have the key to our secret box of emotions, and from time to time, those emotions come up for fresh air and in the process, they betray our true human nature. Whoops!

So, let us deal with the basics before we get into the big league of emotional change. What is an emotion and where do they come from? An emotion can be described simply as a quick bodily or mental reaction to an internal or external event or situation. The emotion we experience is determined by the situation that triggers it. For example, when a person receives good news, they experience happiness but might experience sadness or disappointment at bad news. The intensity of an emotion is based on the meaning that we attach to its cause. Therefore, the same emotion can be experienced differently among people. Finally, the stronger an emotion is, the greater its possible impact.

The human brain is an emotion production facility on steroids. While it is busy keeping us alive and thinking about what we are going to have for dinner next week when our friends come over, among other things, it is also churning out emotions by the millisecond. As a matter of fact, at a subconscious level, emotions are more rapid than conscious thought and do not seek our permission to occur. Fortunately, or unfortunately for us, we are not aware of all the situations that trigger our emotions, but our brains are experts at this as they are always scanning our environment for threats or rewards. Despite our lack of awareness, our emotions play a big role in the decisions that we make, whether we can acknowledge them or not. For example, that dinner menu you were busy thinking about a few sentences ago (or at least now you are) will likely be influenced by how your friends or family reacted to it the last time you made a particular dish and the emotional impact it had on you. Was it yummy? Did it have too much or not enough salt? Or maybe I should just forget about this kitchen thing and just order takeaway?

THE NATURE OF EMOTIONS

It is important to know that emotions are subjective. That is, we experience them in different ways. For example, one person can be angry and only show it by rolling their eyes while another person can go from zero to a hundred in a few seconds and become consumed by rage. Also, emotions are not always as clear-cut as we might think. You might have seen one of a few popular movie scenes where a guy is standing at the altar about to get married and as the bride approaches him to seal the deal, he starts crying. Is he experiencing great joy at being hitched to the love of his life, or is he suffering an internal implosion from the sheer nervousness or doubt about the big decision he is about to make? Maybe he is experiencing both at the same time. We may never know, but for his sake, we hope they are tears of joy.

Our emotions can also cause very strong physiological responses. This means that we feel them physically in our bodies. The absolute fear of speaking in public or even delivering a presentation in front of one other person is enough to reduce someone to pure perspiration or make them run away like they are being chased by a ferocious lion on an African savannah. On the opposite end, when you get near to the person you like or love, especially on those swoony first dates, your heart can forget its blood-pumping purpose and take on the role of a percussive musical instrument that feels like it wants to beat its way out of your chest and into the other person's hands. Emotions are powerful.

> *While we might not possess a mastery of all our thoughts or be bound in fetters by our emotions, our actions can generally indicate our emotional state.*

Everything that we have seen so far about the subjective and physiological aspects of emotions has been based primarily on internal responses and experiences. The final aspect of the emotions that we want to look at is the behavioural response. This is how we choose to express our emotions. Our social and cultural upbringing as well as social context are integral to how we behave in response to the emotions we experience. For example, we might suppress our feelings of anger toward an authority figure like our boss, parent, or pastor but vent our frustration or displeasure (that is, cuss them out) when we're with our friends or by ourselves. This means that we can choose how we react in certain situations based on the potential consequences of the behaviour we show.

By this stage, you are probably wondering if emotions, feelings, and moods are all different words for the same thing, so let us see. From a scientific perspective, they all mean different things. We have seen that emotions are short-lived but intense experiences that result from situations or events around or within us. On the other hand, feelings are influenced by our perception of the situation that caused the emotion in the first place and tend to last longer than emotions. Feelings are reinforced by our thoughts and can be experienced differently by people even when triggered by the same emotion. For instance, let us say a husband and wife have just argued about why the husband has not done the dishes; they both experience anger from the disagreement, but the husband might interpret the situation as the wife being difficult and quarrelsome about a minor chore while the wife feels frustrated about always having to tell her husband (a grown man) to clean up after himself. In both cases, their feelings are different based on their interpretations of the situation. The final term in the affective triad is mood, which can be described as a temporary emotional state, the cause of which may or may not be identifiable. For example, you might be smashing your goals for a few days, and that puts you in a good mood. Or you might start crying if it rains for an extended period, but you do not know why you are sad. If you notice a persistent low mood, it might be time to seek professional help. In short, a good way to help you remember the difference between emotions, feelings, and mood is to remember that they last from shortest to longest in that same order.

THE POWER OF EMOTIONS

If you are someone who does not pay a great deal of attention to your emotions, you might be wondering what the big deal is. For example, you might wonder if it is necessary to develop yourself emotionally, especially if you have managed well enough in your life so far without giving much thought to your emotional side. Well, we have already seen how all humans are emotional beings whether we know it or not. Furthermore, the human brain is more susceptible to emotional manipulation than we think. For example, did you know that it cannot tell the difference between emotions that are experienced, remembered, or imagined? That is, whether we are angry about something, remember feeling angry, or imagined that we are angry, our brain experiences the emotion of anger in a way that is as genuine as the emotion itself. That is why just seeing a picture on social media, hearing a story, or thinking about how someone might have hurt us in the past makes us experience the rage associated with the situation all over again. In that case, Jane's story above might have a similar effect of making someone as angry as they would be if they had been through the hurt and disappointment themselves.

We only need to take a quick look around us to see how the power of emotions is used to influence us in one way or another. Think about billboards, advertisements, social media influencers, and even content creators. Copious amounts of information flood our brains daily, and they all exert an impact on our decision-making processes. For example, seeing our favourite

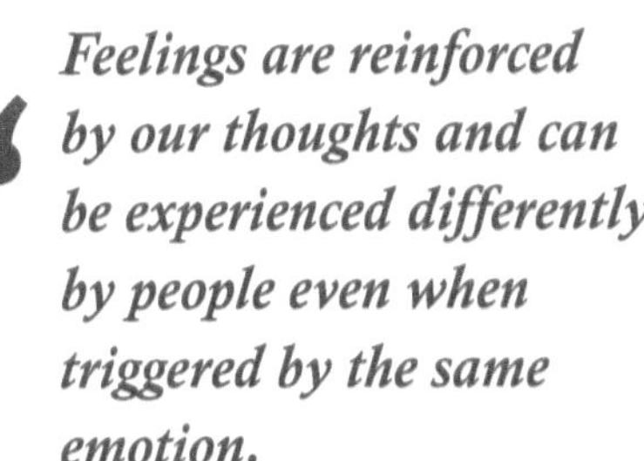

television star advertise a particular fragrance could be enough to make us buy it. Because we hold the person in high esteem and they evoke certain positive emotions in us based on their cinematic performance, we might mindlessly exchange our cash for the perfume, not necessarily due to a personal need but because of our emotional attachment to an imaginary role they play.

Further evidence for the power of emotions comes from different areas of research. Psychologist, Dr Jim Taylor explains how emotions are positioned at the top of the Prime Sports Pyramid, above motivation, confidence, intensity, and focus. This is because emotions determine an athlete's performance during a competition. Specifically, he points out how negative emotions can harm performance both physically, through muscle tension and breathing problems, and mentally, through negative thoughts about the capacity to perform well, leading to a decline in confidence, which all impact one's ability to focus on achieving their goal.

Emotional baggage can also hinder peak performance in cases where negative perceptions of past failures can overshadow present efforts and might even become habits that lead to emotional responses to setbacks. How many times have you seen tennis rackets smashed to pieces on TV? In other spheres of life, research has shown that men are less resilient than women after the loss of a partner and are more likely to die following the death of their spouses. In part, this is due to men having poorer psychological coping mechanisms than women, who are better able to return to a normal life than men. In these cases, men are urged to seek professional help to manage the emotions resulting from the death of a spouse. So then, knowing the potency of human emotions, why should we not learn about how to manage them?

Emotions can be experienced as either anticipatory, in light of a future event taking place, or reactive, occurring after the event has passed. Anticipatory emotions are based on the uncertainty of the future, which humans tend to be terrible at predicting. We experience positive emotions like excitement about an uncertain but positive future event such as a loved one visiting from abroad, but if the uncertainty is negative, then the emotion might be fear or anxiety such as not feeling prepared for an upcoming exam. With reactive emotions, we might experience happiness when our expected visitor arrives where we are, but if the trip is cancelled, perhaps due to inclement weather, then we might experience sadness or disappointment.

There is a famous saying that '*We might be the master of our own thought, still we are the slaves of our own emotions.*' Indeed, while we might not possess a mastery of all our thoughts or be bound in fetters by our emotions, our actions can generally indicate our emotional state. Both anticipatory and reactive emotions can lead to what we call action tendencies. That is, the actions we carry out are based on the emotions that we experience. When the emotions are positive, we are motivated to seek after or maintain the event associated with them, but when they are negative, we are more likely to avoid the event or reduce the discomfort that they bring. This is why we procrastinate in many cases and seek out distractions or more pleasurable activities. This is a major point to bear in mind if you want to be productive in your tasks and purpose. As world-renowned leadership expert, John C. Maxwell, puts it, '*Your attitude determines your actions, and your actions determine your accomplishment.*' Attitude springs from the well of our emotions and our evaluation of the event that provokes the emotion in the first place, concerning our goals. This means that positive emotions lead to the promotion of outcomes while negative emotions lead to their prevention.

Now that we have learnt a little about emotions, where they come from, and how they affect us, next, we will look at how we can get better at understanding and managing them. Since emotions are closely linked to a major aspect of our daily lives and decision-making, we will examine them from that perspective using the real-life story of Jane and her son that we saw at the beginning of this chapter.

DECISIONS: CHANGING THE EMOTIONAL YOU

In Jane's story above, we can see several factors that could be considered from multiple perspectives. To help highlight in practical terms how she escaped from her emotional doldrums and lived a better life for herself and her children, we will consider two key aspects of her story:

1) The night of the heartrending milk mishap.

2) The day she encountered her children's father after more than twenty years.

You might be thinking that Jane had many years to 'get over' her hurt, but as we have seen, to the brain, an emotion experienced because of an event is just as real as one that is recalled from memory. Therefore, Jane could have reacted in a way that could have been considered more proportionate to the pain and anguish that she had felt all those years ago. Furthermore, she could have used all those years to compound hate for the man and despise him even more than she did on the night when he watched her son suck milk from between the cracks on the dirty wooden floor of their cramped room.

CEO of Decisive, a decision sciences company and TEDx speaker, Cheryl Strauss Einhorn, points out in her aptly titled Harvard Business Review article 'Emotions Aren't the Enemy of Good Decision-making' that the difficulty and complexity of the decisions we take are matched in kind with the emotions associated with them. She explains that we often rush through our decisions because we don't want to sit with these uncomfortable feelings, but this usually leads to poor decisions and leaves us feeling worse. Furthermore, it gets us stuck in an unproductive feedback loop which, according to her, bookends our decisions with negative feelings. However, she explains that these emotional bookends can be harnessed to help make better decisions by allowing us to identify two sets of emotions: 1) those that accompany the decision-making action and 2) those that you want to experience as you view your decision retrospectively. The goal is to ultimately identify how your life has benefited from the decision that you end up making. To that end, Cheryl outlines a four-step exercise to allow your thinking, more rational 'wizard brain' to rein in and control your emotional 'lizard brain' to avoid making reactive choices.

1. Identify the decision you need to make

When the milk hit the floor, Jane needed to decide whether to let her son go the night without food and cry himself to sleep or retrieve it from the floor using his mouth. Either decision was a tough one but for different reasons. Seeing her child in pain from hunger was already painful. How much more could she take? When mothers give birth, many are excited about the prospect of breastfeeding to develop that important bond with their children. However, nature doesn't always cooperate and sometimes breast milk can be delayed. In this case, midwives usually advise them that it is better to keep their child alive by giving them a milk substitute such as baby formula than to wait to breastfeed at an undetermined time in the future. Even though this is key to their baby's survival, some mothers are often perplexed by this alternative because breastfeeding carries a certain cultural affirmation, and failure to do so results in feelings of maternal incompetence. In Jane's case, as much as it broke her heart to see him do it, she chose the humiliation of seeing her child feed from the ground like an animal rather than letting him starve.

2. Identify how you feel about the decision you have to make

When Jane saw her children's father after all those years, in the brief moment that it took her to walk toward him, she had to take stock of the flurry of emotions that were erupting inside her. Was she exceedingly bitter from having ruminated for two decades about what she would do or say if this day ever came? Would she feel rejected and scorned all over again, seeing that he had had a good career and had married another woman, and moved on with his life while she suffered alone with their three children? Or was she genuinely happy to see an old friend, no love lost?

3. Visualise your success and how it feels

Jane visualised and executed the success of that night with her son because the decision she took to let him have the milk by any means necessary was, for both of them, a small victory. Tomorrow will take care of itself. Her successes moving forward were about keeping her children alive, giving them a better life, and being emotionally free of all the hurt that converged in her soul that night. So, she also thought long and hard about not binding herself with feelings of resentment and hate toward the man who had abandoned her. She imagined her future, and what kind of mother she wanted to be to her children who still needed her, absentee father or not. She decided that she would push ahead to build a better life for herself and her children and that she needed to be mentally unburdened to accomplish that.

4. Apply the bookends

Jane realised that the anger and sense of hopelessness that she had felt that night were also because of the past failures that she concluded had led to her inability to provide for her children. Some years later after another failed and abusive relationship, Jane hit rock bottom. This time, she sought a way out, permanently. She had made up her mind to commit suicide, but then she had a big moment of clarity just before she tried to drown herself. She thought to herself that she had already overcome so many obstacles with her children, who still needed her. Why should she allow the hurt from another unsupportive man to cause her to abandon her precious children? In that moment, she made up her mind not to seek refuge in the arms of a man but to focus on herself, to develop spiritually, and keep pushing ahead no matter the obstacle on her path. And so, she did. Jane faced every uncomfortable emotion head-on and chose to understand and release them in an emotionally beneficial way. Years later, she married the love of her life, and now almost thirty years later, they're still married and living a happy life together. That was also why when she saw her children's father, she had nothing but love inside her. All the hate had been labelled, processed, and replaced by a more positive emotion.

Your story might be different from Jane's. However, the principles she used to deal with her emotions and make decisions that benefited her and her children many years later are also available to you. You just need to be willing to go through the process of taking back the power from your lizard brain and giving it to your wizard brain. There's no magic in it, just the intentionality of slowing down your reactive decision-making practices, and then identifying and processing your emotions to make better daily decisions.

EMOTIONAL INTELLIGENCE

In this section, you will receive some practical tips to help you navigate the ups and downs of daily life through emotional management and intelligence.

People are intelligent in different ways; for example, some are gifted with numbers, languages, technical skills, etc. These skills often come with experience with content or concepts as people mature and gain more knowledge. However, unfortunately, emotional maturity does not necessarily develop in the same way. For example, a grown person can be the successful CEO of a company but possess very few skills when it comes to managing their own emotions and dealing with problems that arise from their relationship with other people. In short, they lack emotional intelligence (EI). The main thing to know about becoming emotionally mature is that it is not innate but must be learnt by engaging with and interpreting our own emotions.

Emotional intelligence consists of the ability to: 1) Show empathy, 2) Harness emotions for thinking and problem-solving, and 3) Manage emotions (self and others). Here are seven ways to change your emotional self and become more emotionally intelligent:

1) **Get to know yourself** – This goes beyond knowing your favourite foods and digs deeper into who you are as a person. It includes being aware of your values, concerns about the things and people you care about, goals and aspirations, your motivations or fears attached to those, and how willing you are to take risks.

2) **Learn your triggers** – Everything should not have such power over you that you fire off at everyone and everything that does not go your way. Spend time to know what makes you tick and why.

3) **Empathise** – If you are always the most important person in the room and nobody and nothing else matters, you might soon find that you *are* the only person in the room. Learn to see things from other people's perspectives and aim to understand and respect their points of view too, even if you disagree with them.

4) **Ask questions and actively listen** – Mindreading is no longer possible among men, so while you are in this universe of mortals, learn to say what you mean and ask what you do not know. And when you get a response, do not just listen to respond, listen to understand and connect. Ask follow-up questions to ensure comprehension and paraphrase to confirm the interpretation.

5) **Look for body language and other nonverbal signs** – Human beings communicate with a lot more than just our mouths. Our whole body is a communication device, so learn to use and read it well.

6) **Own your emotions and be responsible for how you react to others** – You are not perfect. You might use a word that hurts or do something that someone else does not like. Do not justify bad behaviour, but instead, own your actions and learn to apologise. Your life will be easier.

7) **Recognise that a conversation is a two-way street** – If you insist that your voice alone must be heard, walk away and go have a monologue; it will save you many unnecessary fights. People want to be seen and their voices heard, so if you are not up to it, it is better to keep quiet.

Finally, here are some things that emotionally intelligent people try to do less of:

1. **Criticise others** – It is always easier to say something bad than good about other people. Unfortunately, our brains are programmed to scan our environments for threats at an alarming rate. So, if you have nothing good to say, say nothing.

2. **Worry about the future** – Mark Twain said it best, *'I've lived through some terrible things in my life, some of which actually happened.'* Catastrophizing about the future will never make it better, so do not do it. Plan, prepare, and execute what you can.

3. **Ruminate on the past** – Reflection is good, but it should not be to the point of beating yourself up about your past failures and mistakes. Process your past, learn from it, and keep moving forward.

4. **Maintaining unrealistic expectations** – If you sit under an apple tree, no matter how hard you wish it, the tree will never give you pears. Do not harbour expectations about an impossible future, in the

sincerest meaning of the word. Push your boundaries and strive for excellence always, but do not become a stumbling block in your way and others by being stubbornly inflexible.

Changing the emotional you is a single decision and it starts by looking within. Learn your emotions, then label, process, and engage them. Avoidance will only harm you in the long run – there is no trophy for ignoring your emotions. Remember that your emotions are very real, natural, and common to all human beings, and they are very powerful. It is better to harness them for your benefit than to allow them to run wild and dim the brilliance of your future. If Jane did it, you can too. You can change the emotional you.

CHAPTER 4

CHANGING THE FINANCIAL YOU

By Esther Adeyinka

INTRODUCTION

Have you ever heard the saying, '*Money makes the world go round?*' Well, it is true. As much as we might want to live in a world where money does not matter, unfortunately, that is not the case. Money and its earlier form, bartering, have been around since human beings were able to communicate with each other and form societies. We all understand how it works, right? You work and, in return, you are paid with money. You can then use that money to pay for goods and services. At its core, money is a tool that we use to survive and, in fact, thrive in this world. However, many of us may find that instead of making our money work for us, we are dancing to the beat of money's drum.

Understanding money and learning how to make it work for you is one of the biggest keys to being the complete you. Being able to take control of your finances comes down to a few steps that honestly seem tedious. But often, it's the tedious steps that build the strongest foundations. Everyone owes it to themselves to engage in the tedious and mundane in order to build a strong financial future.

That is what we are going to look at in this chapter - a step-by-step process on how to become the best financial you. We will cover topics like your money story, money habits, financial basics, financial potential, and financial environment.

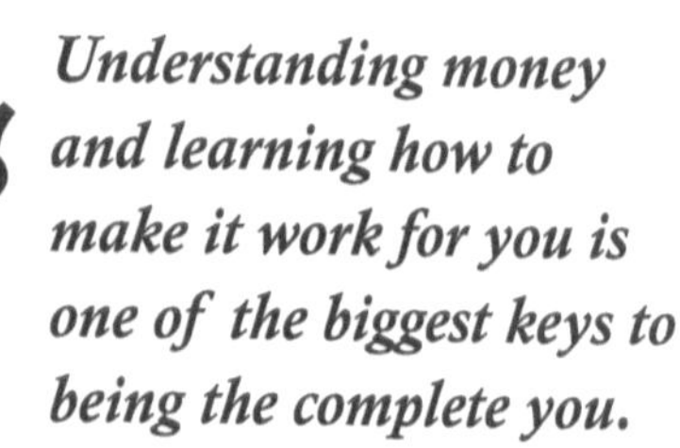

For some of you, this chapter will contain exercises and processes that you have already worked through. For others, you may have never sat down to think or work through any of the steps written here. Both of these cases are perfectly okay. Pick or drop whatever you need to in order to become the best version of yourself.

But before we launch into these different segments, I want to introduce you to two individuals who will accompany us throughout this guide. We will use their lives as case studies to learn from. Firstly, we have Clarissa, a 24-year-old who works as a human resources consultant, loves a good night out with her friends, and is currently in a relationship with her partner, David. Secondly, we have Josh, a 37-year-old husband, and father of two who works as a nurse and loves being creative in his spare time. As we work through each of our steps, we will find out a little more about Clarissa and Josh's lives and see the changes they might need to make in order to be their best financial selves.

STEP 1: UNDERSTAND YOUR MONEY STORY

Before taking a deep dive into some of the changes that can be made to your finances, it is important to take a few steps back and think about a popular concept known as your 'money story.' This is a term coined by the well-known Australian financial expert, Victoria Devine. Your money story simply refers to all the experiences you have had and the behaviours that you have grown up around which relate to money and now influence your relationship with it. Figuring out your money story is an important exercise as it helps to identify important financial experiences that you were influenced by in the past and connect them with your current and future behaviours around money.

Your money story will help you understand why you might see talking about money as something to be afraid of, why you spend money frivolously, or why you don't spend enough money on fun things, even though you might be in a good place financially. Your money story will affect your relationships, your mindset, and your ability to grow financially. Let us take a look at our two individuals and find out more about their backgrounds.

Clarissa grew up in an upper-middle-class family as an only child. Her father and mother never really talked about money, and as far as she was aware, there were no issues with money growing up. She grew up with a generous allowance during her schooling years and was always travelling somewhere during the school holidays with her family.

> *Your money story simply refers to all the experiences you have had and the behaviours that you have grown up around which relate to money and now influence your relationship with it.*

Josh grew up in a low-socioeconomic family of five and was the eldest child. Growing up, he took on a lot of the responsibility in the family home as his parents were often busy working, so he looked after his younger siblings and often found himself planning the grocery list for the week.

Action: Using Clarissa and Josh's examples as a reference point, take a moment and write down the experiences that you had growing up or in recent times that have influenced the way you view and relate to money.

STEP 2: IDENTIFY YOUR MONEY HABITS

Once we have an understanding of our money stories, it is also important for us to identify our money habits. There is a quote that goes something along the lines of, 'a person is the total sum of all their little habits.' This applies to all aspects of life, even to the financial. Your habits when it comes to money will show you what your financial self is.

Admittedly, this is a time-consuming task and actually, for many, a very daunting and messy one. But it is also one that will open your eyes to behaviours and patterns that you may have not noticed before. Financial coaches and experts always recommend that over one night (or a weekend) you take some time to print out the last one to three months' worth of bank statements and read them line by line.

The goal of this exercise is to identify how you spend your money. One way to do this is to take out different highlighters and assign each colour to a different category. For example, one colour for bills, another for groceries, another for going out with friends, and so on. Soon, you will find that a picture of your spending habits will start to emerge. Maybe you will have a lot of green highlights to represent the amount of money you spend on clothes or ordering food.

Clarissa's recent statements show that she spends a substantial amount of money on going out with her friends after work on a weeknight and also during the weekends. Josh's recent statements show that he is extremely frugal; spending only the barest of necessities while saving the remainder.

One really interesting thing about this exercise is that many people will find that their spending habits are often connected to their money story. In Clarissa's instance, she finds herself spending a lot of money on going out to nice restaurants and venues with her friends because growing up, her parents loved to entertain in the same way and her allowance when she was in school included money for going out with her friends. In Josh's instance, we see that there might be a connection between his propensity to be extremely frugal and his experience taking care of most of the household while his parents were at home.

Action: Identify some connections between your current spending habits and your money story.

STEP 3: IDENTIFY THE THINGS THAT 'SPARK JOY'

After going through that activity and seeing the patterns in your spending behaviour, you might think that the next step is to figure out the areas where you need to reduce spending. You would be right in one sense, but before getting there, we need to talk about the importance of having things in your life that 'spark joy.' The idea of sparking joy took the world by storm after its introduction by famous Japanese tidying consultant, Marie Kondo, who specialises in helping individuals tidy up their homes and spaces.

Part of Kondo's five-step method for living an organised life involves getting rid of things that do not spark joy. When working with her clients, before they discard any object, they are asked to consider whether that object 'sparks joy' or not. In essence, is that object something that brings you joy or takes you back to a memorable time? Of course, as Kondo herself says, 'Joy is personal, so everyone will experience it differently.'

Now, here we are not talking about objects specifically, but things or experiences that you spend your money on generally. Before determining whether you need to cut back on certain aspects of your spending, ask yourself whether the spending is something that 'sparks joy.' Of course, be reasonable about it; let us not excuse ourselves from being responsible with our finances, but it's also important to remember that life is for living and living to the fullest.

There are some things that we just cannot afford to do away with, not necessarily because they are essential to life in the way that food, clothes, water, and shelter are, but because they are the things that give us a zest for life. For you, it might be a new outfit now and then because being well-dressed makes you feel confident. Or it may be buying a new PS5 because you love hanging out with your friends through that medium. It may be helping you connect with your inner child. There is absolutely nothing wrong with any of these things, so long as they don't cause you or anyone around you any harm.

Whatever it might be, you may find that it is connected to your money story. For Clarissa, in addition to spending a lot of time going out with her friends, she knows that she also really enjoys buying a pair of beautiful shoes now and then. Of course, they are not necessary, but the level of confidence they give her when she leads meetings at work makes them a thing that 'sparks joy' in her life.

Action: Look through the things you spend a lot of money on and consider whether any of those things 'spark joy'. Why do you think that's the case?

STEP 4: FINANCIAL BASICS FOR SUCCESS

In addition to the things we have talked about earlier, there are a few boring basics that will help you set the foundation for financial success:

Money Mindset

But before we get into those basics, keeping in mind all the things you have identified that spark joy, you need to consider the importance of having a healthy money mindset. I'm hesitant to write about this because often when people talk about having a 'money mindset', they're referring to the mindset you need to have in order to become a millionaire. I cannot count the number of YouTube videos or advertisements I have watched where people talk about a 'millionaire mindset' but come off as a gimmick or as though they are trying to sell you something. But in all honesty, if we take a few steps back and think about it rationally, there is much truth to the idea that the way you think will have an important role to play in determining who and what you become.

There is a famous proverb that says, 'As a man thinks in his heart, so he is,' and it is true. One thing I am very into these days is thinking in what I call a 'delusional mindset.' I realised that the older I got, the more I was slowly letting the hopes and dreams I had as a young person become 'impossible' or 'too hard to achieve.' Of course, some of those goals included things that, in reality, I was not ever going to achieve. But the older you become, the harder you have to work on your mind to truly believe that you can achieve X. I have found out that being a little bit 'delusional' (in the sense of believing even when evidence might show otherwise) when it comes to your dreams can give you the confidence required to chase after those dreams. And as they say, '*Half the battle is in the mind.*'

So, I would like to encourage you to have a healthy money mindset by seeing money as a tool for you to use to help you live your ideal life. Believe that money is not to be feared but rather controlled and directed as you wish.

Discipline

One thing I always try to keep in mind when embarking on a new project or goal is the idea that motivation is fleeting, but discipline is key. Most of us have experienced this before. You come up with a great idea at 3 a.m. and suddenly decide that you want to change your life. For the next few days, you do all the right things: Write up a business plan or start going to bed on time and listening to podcasts in your spare time. But after about a week or two, the business plan has been forgotten, or you are back to your old habits of binging a Netflix show into the early hours of the morning.

It is because we rely on our motivation to get us through, and unfortunately, motivation is a feeling that does not last long. It is the kickstarter for change. But after motivation, you need to practice discipline, something that is honestly quite difficult. Discipline will ask you to put the phone down and turn off the TV at a set time, even though you might have just gotten to a cliffhanger in that show you love. Discipline will ask you to wake up early in the morning to work on that business plan or go for that jog, instead of sleeping for another hour. Discipline is the set of daily tasks that you force yourself to do even when you do not feel like it. And it is the key to building success in any area of your life. Those who are disciplined are more likely to succeed because of the simple fact that they have remained consistent and done the hard work while others gave up after the motivation had left them.

Setting up a Budget - The 50/30/20 Rule

So, armed with your money story and ideas of things that 'spark joy' in your life, here are a few tasks that you can implement that will help you be more disciplined in your financial life. The first is to set a budget. Figure out all your sources of income and how frequently you get paid through those sources. Taking the bank statements that you highlighted earlier, have a look at what it is that you are spending your money on from the time that you get paid up until the next payday. Then set a limit for each area of your life: Rent or mortgage, utilities, groceries, eating out, transportation to and from work, etc. Many tools can help you with setting this up, from a good old Excel spreadsheet (there are even free templates that you can download online) to apps that you can download onto your phone.

If you have never sat down to run a fine-tooth comb through your spending habits, it can be a bit daunting to set your budget. One helpful rule that is used in the traditional finance world is the 50/30/20 rule. The rule asks you to allocate 50 percent of your budget to your needs. This includes things like your food, rent/mortgage, utilities, insurance, and so on. Thirty percent of your budget should then be spent on your wants: Things that are not necessary to your life, but make it easier and more enjoyable. Here is where you can insert some of those things that 'spark joy.' For some people, take Clarissa for instance, it might be a certain amount every month that you get to spend on retail shopping. For others, it might be an amount that can be spent on going out with friends. For you, it might simply be allocating X amount every month to have a streaming service so that you can watch all the latest shows.

The remaining 20 percent is to be apportioned to savings. Almost half of the Australian population finds themselves living paycheque to paycheque, or saving less than 10 percent of their income, meaning that if they were to lose their jobs today, they would have no savings to rely on while they were getting their feet back under themselves. That statistic is caused by a myriad of factors, many of which are outside the control of those living paycheque to paycheque. But if you have the means to do so, then set in place this 20 percent rule.

This rule is a starting point and, of course, can be shifted and moved around depending on your needs.

Paying off Your Debts

There are a few things to take care of as part of your budget. The first is figuring out a way to pay off your debts. Of course, there are good debts and bad debts. For example, credit card debt is almost always seen as a bad debt, whereas a student loan is often seen as a good debt. When we're talking about paying off your debts here, we mean your bad debts first. You may have credit card debts or a 'buy now, pay later' account that you need to pay off. Whatever the case may be, owing money to anyone or any institution restricts how far your entire paycheque can go, so it is a good idea to set aside a little bit of every paycheque to go towards reducing your debt. How aggressive you want to be is up to you.

Some people prefer to repay the lowest amount possible so that, in the immediate term, they can redirect the rest of their funds towards other things that 'spark joy.' Clarissa is one of those people; she has a 'buy now, pay later' account that she uses for her fashion purchases and pays off the minimum amount required every week because she would rather put most of her money toward enjoying the here and now with her friends.

Others may prefer to restrict themselves severely for a short period so that they can pay off debt quickly. In their mind, the quicker they can pay off that debt, the quicker they can get back to spending their money on things that 'spark joy.' Josh is one of those people who prefers to get rid of all of his debt now including his student debts. In addition to the amount taken from his monthly paycheque, Josh also makes additional repayments to his student loan.

You might decide to budget for the debt in the 50% (as a bill) or 30% (as a want) portion of your budget, depending on your point of view. Wherever you land on the spectrum, the important thing is for that debt to be paid off.

Rainy Day Fund

The next thing to take care of in your budget is your 'rainy day fund.' This touches on the issue mentioned above regarding individuals living paycheque to paycheque and the problem that arises if they unexpectedly find themselves out of work or need extended time away from work. Many financial professionals recommend the establishment of a rainy day fund, which aims to build a certain level of savings that can be used for life's unexpected events such as your car breaking down, a large bill, or the loss of your job. One rule of thumb is that you should aim to have the equivalent of three to six months of your salary or wages saved up at any given time. This is probably one of the hardest parts that you will have to enforce and be disciplined about when it comes to your budget. It is hard to put money away and leave it there when there might be a laundry list of things that you want or might even need. However, this is a practice that I promise will give you peace of mind, and that no matter what might happen in the future, you have the means to take care of yourself (and your family as the case may be) financially.

The length of time that it takes you to build up your rainy day fund will vary. If you can only manage to put away $10 a month, then put that $10 away. It might take you two years to build up three months' worth of savings, but the relief you'll have when you hit that goal will be well worth it. This habit should be embedded in the 20% part of the budget rule.

Fun Fund

Another thing to consider is being intentional about setting up a 'fun fund.' This might already fall under your 30 percent of wants, but it can also fall under the 20 percent of savings, particularly for things like travel or big purchases like a designer item or a new piece of technology that you have been eyeing. Drawing again on the need to do things that 'spark joy', sometimes you might need to save up for the things and experiences that will bring you joy when you look at or remember them.

This is something that Josh would be encouraged to implement to ensure that he does not focus so much on saving or paying off debts, to the detriment of having a little fun or joy in his life. Perhaps, he could set up a fun fund for a trip that he might like to take with his partner and kids.

If you have the means, make sure that you include a 'fun fund' in your budget.

Increasing Your Earning Capacity

Earlier, I mentioned that money is a tool to be used to help us live our ideal lives. But there might come a stage in your life where the money you are currently earning just does not allow you to live the kind of life you envision for yourself. This is when you need to start thinking about increasing your earning potential. There are several pathways to doing this.

The first step is taking a look at the work that already pays you, that is, looking at your career. Take some time to assess your skill set, where you are sitting in the business or organisation in terms of hierarchy, and whether there might be room for growth, both in skillset and mainly in terms of salary or wages. While we certainly should not burn ourselves out at work, if you assess where you currently are in your career, you might find that there is room for you to work your way up the ladder and earn more.

If you discover that you might not have the right skill set to work your way up that ladder, then consider whether you have the time and resources to gain extra skills or certifications inside your workplace or outside. If there is no room for growth where you currently are, then you should carefully consider what your other alternatives are; the simplest being changing jobs or maybe even your entire career path.

While waiting for the right opportunity to come up, you can do things like actively learning more in your current role to prepare yourself to get a higher-paying job elsewhere. It is well-known that changing jobs every two to three years is one of the quickest ways to earn more. Of course, that depends on your chosen career.

Start a Business

A lot of us have skills and talents that fall outside of our daily careers, and many of them can be used to help us create extra streams of income through business. If you're someone who loves cleaning, maybe you can start a cleaning service that operates on the weekends or after work hours. If you are great at picking up grammatical errors, perhaps you can spend time in the evenings reviewing people's written work for a fee. Or if you are a fashionista and have a creative streak, you might even consider starting a small clothing line.

All of these ventures will take up a considerable amount of your time and in many cases, money, particularly in the beginning stages. But if you structure your business carefully and establish your expectations from the outset, starting a side hustle might be the thing that helps you save a little more or have more in the bank to spend on things that 'spark joy.' And who knows? You might be one of the many who start a business as a side hustle and end up taking it full-time.

Investing

Another way to increase your earning potential is by making an effort to invest your money in places that will yield good returns. This guide is not aimed at providing investment advice. For that, you really should talk to a professional, but investing is one of the simplest things you can do to secure your financial future. Depending on where in the world you find yourself, you might be able to add to your employee super or retirement funds. You should also consider doing things like apportioning a part of your savings budget (the 20 percent) to investing in stocks.

There are so many innovative apps in the market right now that make investing very simple. Some of them will connect to your bank account, and for every purchase you make, they will round up the number so that the difference in the amount is used to invest. Others will allow you to set a fortnightly or monthly goal that can be used. Another thing you can invest in is property, and these days, you no longer need to purchase a whole property by yourself. You can also put money in with other people to purchase a property together.

STEP 5: PEOPLE YOU ARE AROUND

'Show me your friends and I will show you who you are.' is an old adage, but a truthful one. The next step in crafting a strong financial future for yourself is to assess the people in your inner circle and anyone who influences the way you live your life. You need to be as ruthless with the company you keep as you are with your budget. Constantly auditing your circle is a habit that I recommend everyone embed into their lives.

In this context, you should consider the ways your friends might be influencing your financial habits, mindset, and potential. Are you spending too much time with people who blow all their money on a Saturday night out? Or are you surrounded by people who will do anything to watch the latest season of a movie or show? This is something that Clarissa will particularly need to be aware of, given that she spends a considerable amount of time with her friends. There is nothing wrong with wanting to have a good time or nice things, but not at the expense of blowing the budget you have worked so hard to draw up. If you need to distance yourself from people like that, then please do. Be disciplined about it.

The next level of this step is to surround yourself with people who are headed in the same direction as you or have reached the financial goal that you are aspiring to. This can be a little difficult because people generally are not forthcoming about their financial habits and situation, but if you observe people and their habits, you will start to pick up little signs here and there that will clue you into the relationship that people around you have with money.

STEP 6: TELL YOUR MONEY STORY

This next step is connected to the previous one and it involves telling your money story. This might seem like an odd thing to do, but think of it like this: When you tell the people who care about you what your goals or issues are and the reasoning behind them, they are more likely to understand why you might act or behave in a certain way.

Similarly, by explaining to your carefully audited circle of friends what your money story is, they will be better placed to understand your spending habits. Of course, you can sit down and explain to them what your story is. But if that seems like a bit too much for you, you can just feed your story into daily interactions. For example, you might be like Josh who, because of his family situation, wasn't able to explore his creative side as much because it required money that was not available at the time. Josh would be advised to share his passions with his partner or close friends so that they can help encourage him to put more money aside to pursue his creativity.

STEP 7: ACCOUNTABILITY PARTNERS

By telling your money story, you might also find yourself explaining the financial goals that you have set for yourself and indirectly finding some accountability partners.

Let us get this straight, you are your biggest cheerleader, and you must be because most people are way too busy with their own lives and problems to carry your issues or goals with you. However, if you have done the work to surround yourself with good people, they will be willing to help you some part of the way.

If you tell your family and friends that you can only spend $X amount on going out every week, then those who are your true friends will not force you to go out to places that fall outside of that budget. By being open about your money story and struggles, you might even find that your friends tell you theirs. And really, life is much better when you are walking with other people of a similar mind.

84

CONCLUSION

This concludes the short step-by-step guide to a better financial you. As mentioned at the start of this chapter, this guide is made for you to pick and choose the steps that apply to you. I hope that by reading through this, you have been able to either confirm that you are on the right track as it pertains to the financial you or have highlighted the areas in your life where you might need to make adjustments to your finances.

CHAPTER 5

CHANGING THE PHYSICAL YOU

By Tolu Oliaku

INTRODUCTION

Change does not have to start with a New Year's resolution. It can start with something as little as one lifestyle change at a time. Change can be overwhelming, especially if we try to make a drastic change over a short period. Change requires resisting well-established behavioural patterns, which means that you will be working against unconscious, automatic processes in the brain that are designed to make life easier.

Change is naturally more difficult as we age, but it's beneficial to our general health to encourage it. According to neuroscience, our brain is trained to like familiarity. According to Neurologist Santosh Kesari (MD, Ph.D.), our brain is completely malleable and experiences new things all the time. It has to figure out how to filter out the positive and negative behaviours to choose what is good for survival, and what is not. As we grow older, our brain learns ways to do certain tasks with repetition and behaves accordingly to each context and stimulus. Essentially, it likes positive behaviours which explains why introducing new behavioural modes becomes challenging.

Let us take my journey, for instance. I was raised in a family of sporting stars. Four of my siblings have played basketball in the United States all on scholarships, including myself. This did not come easy as I had to make myself uncomfortable in order to grow. My routine had a disruptive change. This resulted in me having to be in bed at a reasonable time. I wake up by 7:30 a.m., shower, eat, dress up, and walk to school. This was a

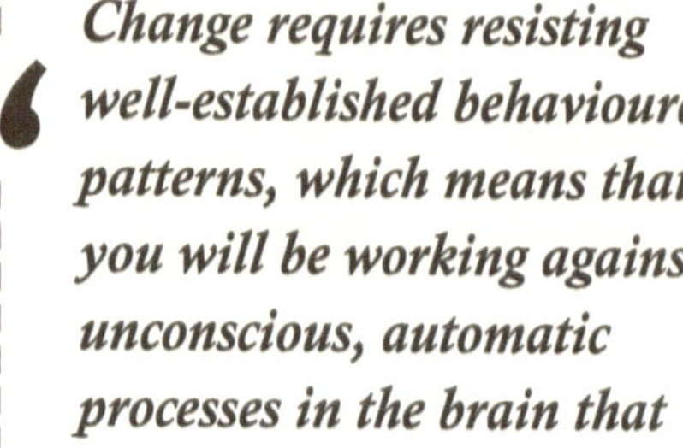

repetitive norm that my body was initially not accustomed to, but years later, as life progressed, I was accepted and awarded a scholarship into a prestigious, yet structured boarding school in the United States. I attended Montverde Academy, a college preparatory school that groomed notable sporting stars such as Ben Simmons, a professional Australian basketball player, D'Angelo Russell, the second overall pick in the 2015 NBA draft, Precious Ezinna Achiuwa, a Nigerian power forward for the Toronto Raptors, Femi Akinpetide, my talented brother who entered the NBA draft in 2013, and many other stars like Sherrexcia Rolle Attorney, a singer, and the first-ever black female to run a black-owned airline. She accomplished all these before the age of thirty.

The day I received my acceptance letter into the Academy, my whole life changed. I was living every athlete's dream. I was one step closer to the American dream. It all seemed too good to be true. I had only dreamt of moving to the United States, but I never thought that speaking my goal into existence would change my whole life.

It all started on just a regular old-school day. I had just transitioned from a public school to a private Catholic school. I disliked every bit of it because I was now in the upper-class region where the more affluent the people were, the less amiable they became. I wasn't accustomed to this because I had always been a standout everywhere I went, mainly because of my height. I am 6'1 feet tall which is well above average for a female. A majority of people's initial reaction to me is either 'She is intimidating', or 'She is too tall.' Neither was the case. I was bullied. For the first time in my life, a bold person actually approached me at my desk, took my seat, threw all my books on the floor, and boldly said, '*You cannot sit here.*' I was so angered that day, but before any words came out of my mouth, a classmate pulled me away, grabbed my books, and told me to walk off because she was going to handle the situation. She calmed me down and reminded me of how hard my father had worked to send me to my first-ever private school and how it wasn't easy. She then said I should not retaliate because if I got suspended, my father would be ashamed.

To this day, I thank that friend of mine. The reason is that it made me hold my tongue and go into deep thought. My thoughts were negative and out of anger. After class, I said I hated it there and I was moving out of there. My friends consoled me saying it was because I was a new student and it was a new environment. They encouraged me to push through because things would get better. I had so much anger built up inside of me that I promised I was leaving that country and moving to America.

They knew there was a zero percent chance of this happening and there was no way I would live over there at the age of 15 without my parents, but just like the saying, *'Be careful what you wish for because you just might get it.'* I spoke what I thought was a joke into the atmosphere and it manifested within hours. To this day, it still seems like a fairy tale, but it is the 100% truth. Less than five hours later, I got a call that changed my whole life and shaped me into the woman I am today. All I remember from the call was, *'Congratulations, you have been accepted into Montverde Academy. Everything is sorted. We have provided a host family for you to live with on weekends. You will be living on campus. Your $30, 000 tuition has been paid in full and we are waiting on you because school has started.'* It all sounded like a joke to my friends the next day. They weren't sure if I had become delusional overnight and thought that this was all just a made-up story. Reality hit everyone two months later when, to my surprise, my parents paid for my flights, and my sister and I said goodbye to friends and family in Australia, at the ages of 12 and 15, we took on our journey to a better opportunity.

This is where the transformation started. My goal of playing basketball at a competitive level started immediately and reality hit. My attitude changed, my posture straightened, and my demeanour lightened up. I went from growing up very insecure to walking around with my nose in the air. This was because I was a minority and I stood out. I saw myself as oversized, big-footed, and a good-for-nothing athlete. I was the only nonathletic child in my family and had to work ten times harder to even be considered for a sporting team. I hated it but trained my brain to turn the negative into positives. Every time one door shut, I analysed the scenario in my head and pushed myself to give it another go.

The most inspirational story that shaped my childhood life is that of the tortoise and the hare. Why? Because I was the tortoise. For those of you who have not read the fable, I would recommend it. The Tortoise was the underdog in the story, the odds were against him for winning the race. The hare, on the other hand, had everything working in his favour. He was fit and had all the right qualities to win the race, but he was overly confident and careless. His carelessness caused him to become lazy, whereas the tortoise put in the extra work. He didn't take shortcuts, naps, breaks, pit stops, or lose sight of the goal. Even though he was outclassed in speed, the tortoise focused on the finish line and remained steady and consistent in a motion that moved forward which led him to win the race.

This reminds me of myself because I knew that I was not as explosive as Nneka Ogwumike, the WNBA explosive star out of Los Angeles, or the female version of Micheal Jordan, but I sure did set my mind to believe I was. While my competitors were sleeping, I was up putting in the physical work. At the age of thirteen, I was up at 4:30 a.m. some days psyching myself up and mentally preparing my mind for a 6 a.m. intense basketball training session, along with my siblings at the Burwood PCYC located in the Inner West of Sydney.

We travelled by train, trained for one hour, showered, and rushed back via public transport to start school by 9 a.m., then finished school by 3 p.m. and headed back to training. At the time I was going through this, I wondered if it was worth it. But I stayed curious and determined. It became a habit and I began to see positive changes. I was getting physically and mentally stronger and the excess weight I was not pleased with started shedding off naturally. I became confident and started building an image for myself. I was no longer oversized and good for nothing. I was now Tolu Akinpetide, the high school star basketballer averaging roughly 16 points a game and the biggest threat in every sport I attempted. This was the confidence I needed to kick start my desire to be everything people said I was not. It was my duty to unlearn a lot of my social norms and set my mind to a structured environment. This was the biggest change I had ever experienced and, of course, the change was not just physical, it was spiritual and psychological too.

Physically, I slimmed down and toned up due to the amount of physical activity I was engaging in. Spiritually, I had to find a means of mental stability through prayers, quiet time outs, worshiping, and bible reading to encourage me not to give up, and psychologically, I had to find ways to emotionally keep myself afloat and committed. Anybody can change but the question is, what will drive them to change? Change is often complicated, and it does not always happen the way you envision it, but the following reminders can help you maintain a realistic perspective about the process.

WHAT YOU SHOULD KNOW ABOUT CHANGE

Change cannot be forced, it needs to be agreed upon within. We have to remember that we cannot control anyone's actions. It is a decision that must be made personally. Change takes time and effort. It is important to set realistic goals for yourself and understand the decision behind the goal. For example, not eating after 6 or 7 pm, or not showing up late. These are goals that have action steps that you can work towards over time. Do not expect overnight progress. My basketball journey took four years. I slowly, but steadily paced myself. I even drew out vision boards and worked toward them. Remember that change does not take a linear path, it is non-linear, meaning it is not a straight line or path. Nothing great comes without adversity and pain tolerance.

I recently listened to a podcast with Tim Grover, Kobe Bryant, and Michael Jordan's sports enhancement specialist and performance expert who helped lead them to their legendary status. Mr Grover says that to reach greater heights as an athlete or successful person, you have to know your pain tolerance. You must understand pain coupled with knowing your tolerance towards the pain. The more you understand this, the more it will cause you to be successful. You can use pain to excel or surrender.

Trauma causes greatness, it also causes despair. You need to ask yourself if you are interested in what you are doing or if you are obsessed. You cannot be both. Kobe Bryant was not interested in winning the number one title, he was obsessed. Interested people watch obsessed people change the world. Do not be that person. Maximise your focus so it can give you more time. Did you know that before a game, Kobe Bryant and his mentor, Tim Grover, would walk around the court with a basketball trying to find dead spots on the wooden floor? Once they found the dead spot, Kobe would force his defender into the dead spot which gave him a competitive edge. There was even a game where Kobe started throwing free throws before the game and turned to the court maintenance guy to ask if he was sure that the basket was positioned right. The guy said it was right then he pulled out a measuring tape to measure and prove his point. It just so happened that Kobe's observation was right. It was an eighth of an inch off from being in the right position.

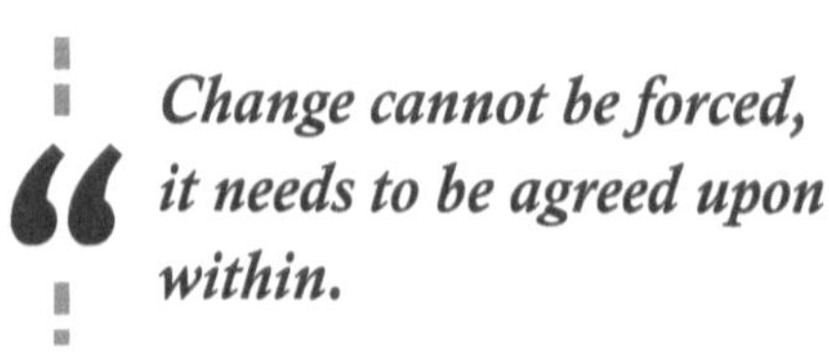

Grover says Kobe's vision was to be the best and to reach his goal, he had to come out of his comfort zone. When you want to reach your goal and succeed, you have to pay attention to details. The most successful individuals struggle with balance. You cannot be the best at one thing and then try to balance the other and expect the same result. You have to channel your focus. Let the dark side be the driving force in your life. In my instance, being big and overweight was my driving force. Nothing great comes without adversity and pain tolerance.

The more you understand what caused you the pain and how you dealt with it, the more this will help you to determine how successful you will be in life.

> **"** *Nothing great comes without adversity and pain tolerance. The more you understand what caused you the pain and how you dealt with it, the more this will help you to determine how successful you will be in life.*

See, I physically had to go through the pain to see the results I wanted. I had to train through rain, hail, shine, blood, sweat, and tears. Was it worth it? Yes! Why? Because it shaped me to be a better person. I put constant pressure on myself to reach my goal of playing at a collegiate level because I chose to. I admit that I wasn't the best player out there. I was criticised, doubted, given up on, replaced, and cut from multiple sporting teams, but through all the adversity, my state of mind was strengthened and I became tougher. Not only did it shape me for the next phase in my life, but I also changed physically. I was in the best shape of my life. I had so much lean muscle and the percentage of fat in my body was almost at the professional athlete level. I looked good, and I carried myself with high esteem. I did not look down as I walked, instead, I looked up and kept my crown held high. I was even crowned the first-ever Miss International Queen on my campus and given multiple scholarships due to my work ethic and composure.

THE KEY TO CHANGING THE PHYSICAL YOU

The key is to set realistic goals. Military workouts three times a day are not realistic. Have a goal in mind and find ways to get there. For example, if you have tried running, or even tried weightlifting and found that you are getting bored, throw in something more realistic like a 30-minute walk each day while listening to your favourite podcast. You could even join a team sport. Team sports helped me out a lot because it gave me the feeling of a shared goal where each person carried their weight toward a shared goal. You also have to remember not to be too hard on yourself. After all, Michael Jordan once said, '*I have missed more than 9,000 shots in my career. I have lost almost 300 games. 26 times, I have been trusted to take the game-winning shot and missed. I have failed over and over and over again in my life.*'

Michael Jordan also said, '*If you're trying to achieve, there will be roadblocks. I've had them; everybody has had them. But obstacles don't have to stop you. If you run into a wall, don't turn around and give up. Figure out how to climb it, go through it, or work around it.'*

As Carol Dweck, author of Mindset, would say, Jordan is a prime example of the growth mindset. It is the mindset that almost every successful athlete who has had long-term success has. He said, '*Genetics may determine the starting line, but hard work determines the finish line.*'

In changing the physical you, we are referring majorly to generally living a more healthy and productive life. This does not just happen by itself. There are steps you must take to make it a reality that is rooted in a better understanding of the factors that make healthy living possible. Let's go deeper into that.

BREAKING UNHEALTHY HABITS

According to the Australian Government, multimorbidity, which is the presence of two or more chronic illnesses at a time, is more common among females than males. And over 1 in 3 (33%) aged 15 or over with multimorbidity experience high or very high psychological distress.

Causes Of Chronic Diseases

Many chronic diseases are caused by a short list of risk behaviours:

- Tobacco use and exposure to secondhand smoke.

- Poor nutrition, including diets low in fruits and vegetables and high in sodium and saturated fats.

- Lack of physical activity

- Excessive alcohol use

Let us touch on nutrition. Having the right balanced diet is crucial in this day and age. I have had my fair share of asthma attacks due to poor diet and artificial additives to the foods I ate as a child. I recall having breathing difficulties if I consumed excess sugary foods and drinks. At one point, I was even asked to stay away from any food that contained red food colouring because it triggers an attack. Another trigger was second-hand smoke. My parents recently took me down memory lane on my trip to Africa on a plane where smoking was allowed. Not long into the flight, an emergency broke out in my body and my airways started to cave in and I was not able to breathe. The flight attendants came over and I was given a nebulizer and medication to assist with my breathing. The good news is that the attendants were able to speak to the second hand smokers and pleaded with them to stop smoking. Two years later, a law was passed to stop smoking on a plane. Where am I getting at with this? There are so many chain reactions in our bodies. Care must be taken and a lifestyle change is needed in order to avoid falling into the chronic disease bracket.

Your diet is partly responsible for 30 to 40 percent of all cancer, but nutrition alone cannot cause or cure cancer It is important to understand the foods that contribute to cancer or other conditions that change the physical you.

Below are some foods to avoid

1.) Processed meats

According to the U.S. Department of Agriculture, Americans are eating more meat than ever, around 222 pounds each year, per person. Processed meats including sausage, hot dogs, pepperoni, packaged lunch meat, beef jerky, ham, and bacon may increase the odds of developing colorectal cancer. The World Health Organization warns that daily consumption of even one hot dog or a few strips of bacon increases cancer risk by 18%. Processed meats are any that have been cured, smoked, salted, canned, or dried. They contain nitrates, preservatives added to enhance flavour and deter bacteria growth. Nitrates also occur naturally in fresh foods. Researchers can anecdotally link them to cancer, though the research is inconclusive and ongoing.

2.) Hot beverages

Shockingly enough, according to the International Journal of Cancer, hot beverages higher than 140 degrees Celsius cause thermal damage to the cells that line the esophagus and may be responsible for the increased risk of cancer. Those who consume alcohol and smoke cigarettes increase their chances of developing esophageal cancer fivefold

3.) Overcooked and burnt food

Some overcooked or burnt foods, mainly meat, form

chemicals called heterocyclic amines (HCAs) or polycyclic aromatic hydrocarbons (PAHs). These chemicals are the result of amino acids, sugars, and creatinine reacting at high temperatures. The juices that drip down onto an open flame or heat source create smoke that releases PAHs, which then adhere to the surface of the meat. Meats cooked at temperatures of 300 degrees Fahrenheit or above or those meats cooked for very long periods, form HCAs. Acrylamides form when starchy foods cook until they are dark brown. Some studies link the consumption of these compounds to ovarian and endometrial cancers, though definitive evidence is still lacking.

4.) Alcoholic Beverages

Even small amounts of alcohol increase the risk of developing cancer. According to the American Cancer Society, alcohol consumption is linked to 5.6% of all new cancers and 4% of cancer deaths. Heavy or regular alcohol use also increases the likelihood of developing cancer of the mouth, pharynx, larynx, oesophagus, liver, colon, and rectum. Genetics plays a role in a person's chances of developing cancer as a result of drinking alcohol. Genes encode the enzymes involved in metabolising alcohol. Individuals of East Asian heritage may carry a version of the gene that speeds the conversion of alcohol to a toxic chemical called acetaldehyde. Those who carry this gene have a higher chance of developing oesophageal cancer.

5.) Dairy

Milk and other dairy products like cheese are high in saturated fat and cholesterol, but studies show that the calcium they contain may lower the risk of colorectal and other types of cancer. However, a high intake of dairy products may increase the possibility of prostate cancer. According to the Physicians Health Study, a 28-year study of more than 21,000 people shows that subjects who consumed more than 2.5 servings of dairy products each day were more likely to develop prostate cancer.

6.) Refined Carbohydrates and Sugars

People who eat a diet high in refined carbohydrates such as white bread, white rice, pasta, soft drinks, and fruit juices are more likely to develop colon cancer than those who consume mostly whole grains and complex carbohydrates such as fresh vegetables and fruits. Studies support the probability that high blood glucose and insulin levels in the body increase inflammation and along with it, the risk of cancer. The glycaemic index measures how fast carbohydrates turn into sugar in the blood. A 2016 study linked excess consumption of high glycaemic index foods to an 88% greater risk for prostate cancer.

7.) Salt-Cured and Pickled Foods

Cancer studies in the United Kingdom note a higher incidence of nasopharyngeal cancer among those who regularly consume salt-cured fish, a popular dish in China.

Research also indicates that eating pickled foods may increase the risk of stomach cancer. According to a study in the *American Association for Cancer Research* journal, of the 1 million new cases of gastric cancer diagnosed each year, more than half occur in Eastern Asia. Researchers noted a 50% greater likelihood of gastric cancer associated with the consumption of pickled foods, with a higher number of cases in China and Korea.

8.) Red Meat

Studies show eating more than 18 ounces of red meat per week can increase the chance of colorectal cancer. Some studies also link processed meats with a higher incidence of colon cancer. Doctors suggest introducing meat-free days and generally cutting back on the amount of red meat consumed. People should avoid overcooking red meat, which produces chemicals that may increase the risk of colorectal cancer.

9.) Microwave Popcorn

Popcorn is a fibre-rich, low-fat, healthy snack, but it comes with some caveats. The lining of the bag used to make microwave popcorn contains perfluorinated compounds (PFCs) to resist grease and prevent leaking. PFCs also exist in Teflon pans, pizza boxes, and sandwich wrappers. These PFCs break down into a chemical some researchers believe causes cancer. A majority of Americans have PFCs in their blood, so research is ongoing to figure out how they relate to disease and what level of harm they carry. According to the

U.S. Food and Drug Administration, microwave popcorn accounts for more than 20% of the PFOA levels in Americans.

10) Food Dyes

For many years, there has been a controversy surrounding the use of food dyes. Many studies show many dyes adversely affect laboratory animals. As a result, government agencies have banned several types. The Food and Drug Administration has approved nine food dyes for use in the U.S., including Red No. 3, Red No. 40, Yellow No. 5, and Yellow No. 6. Health researchers and food safety officials express concerns over their continued use, but manufacturers continue to add them to candies, sports drinks, baked goods, salad dressings, and even medications. Research indicates these dyes contain carcinogens and cause cancer in lab animals. As these dyes do not enhance the nutritional quality or safety of foods or medications, scientists continue to argue that they should not be added to food products.

And the list goes on.

The Effects of Proper Nutrition on the Body

- A Healthy Heart. By lowering your intake of fats, sodium, and cholesterol, you can help your heart stay healthy.

- A Healthy Mind.

- Healthy Teeth and Bones.

- More Energy.

- Managing Weight.

- Hunger Management.

- Foster Growth.

- Longer Lifespan.

HOW CAN WE DO BETTER?

Eating inadequate amounts of protein, or eating the wrong proteins can lead to muscle wasting, a poor immune system, lacklustre energy, and liver problems. Your body uses the protein you eat to build muscle, repair damaged tissue, form immune and blood cells, make hormones, and synthesise

Be Active

Did you know that according to the CDC, there are 13 cancers associated with a high Body Mass Index including thyroid, gallbladder, colon, and breast cancer?

Following dietary guidelines for adequate nutrition and aiming for at least 150 minutes of exercise a week are simple things everyone can do to reduce their risk of obesity-related cancer.

Ironically enough, if exercise was a pill, it would be the most popular pill in the world that is worth nothing. The myriad benefits of running once a week is so beneficial to not just your body, but your mind. Many people seem to think that the only benefit that running has brought them is losing weight. I want us to shift our biased beliefs and understand the anatomy and physical makeup of our bodies.

Running for at least 10 minutes a day can **significantly lower your risk of cardiovascular disease**. Runners lower their chances of dying from heart disease by half. It also lowers your resting heart rate (the number of times your heart beats per minute when you're at rest). According to an article from love life be fit Running boosts your cardio, helps reduce stress, and lets you sleep well at night.

Taking up running is good for your fitness and can help you lose weight.

Expect to lose body fat and develop enviable calf muscles. I found out that running is a form of therapy. Whenever I am in a stressed state of mind, I pop my air pods in and go for a slight jog. I feel the worrying of my mind disappear and my mind focuses more on pleasant things.

Running outside has many benefits such as exposure to Vitamin D.

According to the National Institute of Health Vitamin D promotes calcium absorption in the gut and maintains adequate serum calcium and phosphate concentrations to enable normal bone mineralisation and to prevent hypocalcemic tetany (involuntary contraction of muscles, leading to cramps and spasms). It is also needed for bone growth and bone remodelling by osteoblasts and osteoclasts. Without sufficient vitamin D, bones can become thin, brittle, or misshapen. Vitamin D sufficiency prevents rickets in children and osteomalacia in adults. Together with calcium, vitamin D also helps protect older adults from osteoporosis.

Vitamin D has other roles in the body, including the reduction of inflammation as well as modulation of such processes as cell growth, neuromuscular and immune function, and glucose metabolism. Many genes encoding proteins that regulate cell proliferation, differentiation, and apoptosis are modulated in part by vitamin D. Many tissues have vitamin D receptors, and some convert 25(OH)D to 125(OH)2D.

To sum up the above, in order to change the physical you, it is critical to set achievable goals (You can use aids such as setting goals for lifestyle change), incorporate 30 minutes of exercise daily, break unhealthy eating habits, minimise processed foods, and eat meals that are not overcooked so you don't lose the essential nutrients, try to avoid refined sugars, excessive alcohol, and simply just stick to a balanced diet.

CHAPTER 6

CHANGING THE SOCIAL YOU

By Mofoluwaso Ilevbare

You probably have heard the saying before, '*You may never appreciate what you have until you lose it*.' I had that experience about three years ago when I relocated with my family to Australia, a completely different culture and different weather conditions - a new way of life. One of the first things that made me homesick was the fact that my daily conversations were reduced to the barest minimum in the first few weeks. Born and raised in Africa, 'Good morning', and 'How was your night?' are common phrases you'd probably get asked ten times before you get to the office. It's likely to come from your family members, the security guard, the gardener, the neighbour washing his car, and even the people standing by the newspaper vendor. When you get to the office, you are likely to get asked the same or similar questions by the security personnel and one or two colleagues. Moving to a new office, the regular banter and small talk gradually became memories, replaced by the awkward pauses and stares you get when building new relationships in unfamiliar terrain.

Barely three months in our new home, the COVID-19 pandemic hit - a global epidemic that spread rapidly, impacting the way we worked and lived. Due to the alarming spread and rise in deaths, the government put in stricter measures of lockdowns, and isolation periods, including the 5 km distance limitation outside of your residence. For a family like ours which had barely made any friends nor established a strong support system, the isolation was a big blow to our social life. We barely received a call or a check-in to see if we were okay. The only comfort was from a few work colleagues in my team. When I managed to go out for morning walks, it was funny to see how awkwardly we all kept the 1.5m distance as per regulations. People changed their pace and stared with anxiety whenever they saw anyone else coming close. It was a bizarre time.

Moving to a new country was not strange to me. After all, this was our fifth relocation in fifteen years. I longed for the warmth of family and friends, the smiles of strangers in the shops, and small talk at the local cafés. These were quickly replaced with Zoom meetings and in most cases, with cameras turned off. I found myself in an environment where people hardly said a word to each other along the streets, hardly smiled at strangers, and hardly reached out as a neighbour. This was a tough thing to adjust to.

Have you ever been in a social situation where things looked unfamiliar, you felt you didn't know what to say, or maybe said something that came across the wrong way? I have been there too. One skill I have developed over the years that keeps me going in new environments is *learning how to create my inner 'sunshine,' nurture it, carry it around, and make it contagious.* Human beings were created to thrive in social settings. Communities are built on relationships and social interactions, culture, and the ability to reproduce. Developing your social skills and expanding social networks have far-reaching benefits in your personal and professional lives. I'd refer to it as what psychologists call social intelligence.

WHAT IS SOCIAL INTELLIGENCE?

Have you ever observed individuals who can smoothly engage in conversation with anyone they meet, regardless of their varying backgrounds? Conversely, have you encountered someone who consistently offends others regardless of the subject matter? These two scenarios illustrate how our aptitudes for communication, camaraderie, and empathy with those around us can differ. Similar to traditional academic competencies, we possess differing levels of social intelligence. This social competence has been the subject of extensive academic research and is now commonly recognised as an essential skill.

Social intelligence is distinct from other types of intelligence such as IQ and EQ (emotional intelligence). Daniel Coleman, in his book, *Social Intelligence*, refers to this terminology as the ability to perceive and understand the emotions others display and to use this information to interact effectively with them. It is the ability to understand

and navigate social situations in your personal and professional life, communicating effectively in a way that brings out the best outcome. A socially intelligent person displays a high level of awareness, self-confidence, charisma, and empathy which are essential for building and maintaining social relationships.

In today's hyper-digital age, people tend to think it is easier to develop the 'social you.' From borderless social media apps to pop-up notifications – keeping you up-to-date with the latest trends and news; influencers and celebrities shaping culture – it seems easier to become liked and loved and popular, finding your self-worth in the number of followers and likes, yet hiding the truth about yourself behind the camera. On the other hand, engaging in social media can be overwhelming for others who cannot seem to connect with people beyond face value.

However, research shows that people with high social intelligence are more likely to be successful in their careers than those with high IQ or EQ alone. This is because social intelligence is essential for effective leadership, teamwork, and communication. Socially intelligent individuals possess a unique ability to empathise with others, effortlessly navigate social situations, and exude confidence in larger groups. Although commonly referred to as 'people skills,' the true descriptor for this talent is social intelligence. First introduced by the American psychologist Edward Thorndike in 1920, social intelligence is defined as the capacity to comprehend and manage human interactions with wisdom.

This quality is not innate but rather a learnt skill set that takes time to develop. People with high social intelligence are better able to form strong, positive relationships with others, which can lead to greater happiness and fulfillment in life. In contrast, people with low social intelligence may struggle to form and maintain relationships, leading to loneliness and isolation.

DEVELOPING SOCIAL INTELLIGENCE

Social intelligence can be improved with training and practice (Mayer & Salovey, 1997). This means that anyone can improve their social intelligence, regardless of their starting point. Let me tell you about my friend, Troy. Troy is a young, brilliant lawyer working at a top law firm, and recently won a major case that has brought him into the limelight, a good one for his budding career. When I met with him to congratulate him, he had this nagging feeling he couldn't shake off. He had been so focused on winning case after case that he barely had a social life. I encouraged him to chat with his mentor and take it from there.

A few weeks later, Troy was leaving the courthouse when he ran into Olivia, his mentor, and one of the top lawyers in the city. *'Nice job in there, kid,'* Olivia said with a smile. *'But you don't look excited for someone who just won a case. Walk with me. What's eating you up?'*

Troy hesitated for a moment before admitting,

'I love my job, but I'm afraid I might end up dying alone if I don't get my social life in order. I can argue cases and cite legal precedents, but when it comes to finding love and building real friendships, I can't seem to get it together.'

Olivia leaned in and said, *'Look, Troy, being a lawyer isn't just about knowing the law. It's about understanding people, their motivations, their fears, and their desires. You have a bright career ahead of you and a ton of people who would love to be your real friends. Why don't you come over to my house tonight — I'm hosting an exclusive networking event. Maybe you'd make a few new friends.'*

'It's not my thing. I hate small talk,' Troy protested.

Olivia grinned. *'Small talk is a skill, kid. The secret to enjoying small talk is to improve your listening skills and care that the other person carries value.'*

At the event that night, Troy felt out of place. He saw a few familiar faces from the legal world but didn't feel like engaging. He was about

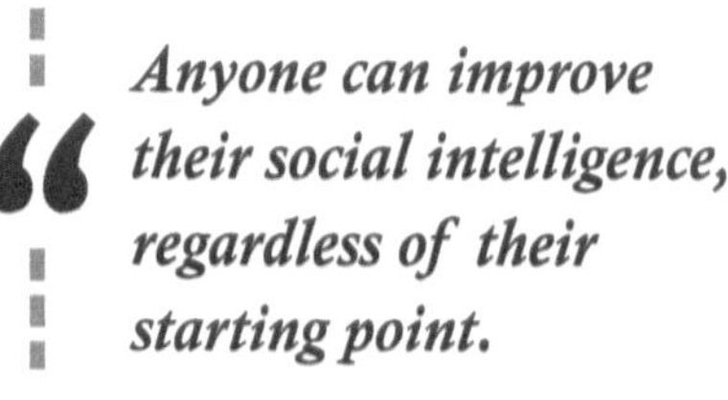

to give up and go home when he saw someone sitting quietly by the bar, all by himself, sipping a mocktail. He could almost hear Olivia's voice in his head, so he decided to take a chance and approached him.

'Hi, I am Troy. What brings you here tonight?'

The other gentleman smiled and introduced himself as Bode, a highly respected statesman. They struck up a conversation about their work, their hobbies, and their favourite TV shows. Troy found himself enjoying the conversation and Bode seemed to be genuinely interested in what he had to say. They were joined by two other people and had a great time of fun and laughter. When Troy was leaving the event, he saw Bode again.

'Hey, Bode, it was great talking to you. Let us grab lunch sometime and continue our conversations .'

Troy felt a surge of confidence. He had taken a step outside his comfort zone, and it had paid off. He had made a new connection, and who knew where it could lead? Over the next few weeks, Troy practiced his social skills every chance he got. He went to more networking events, struck up conversations with strangers at the coffee shop, and even volunteered at a local charity event. He found that the more he practiced, the easier it became. And as he honed his social skills, Troy realised that he was not only winning more cases, but his confidence was also rising and so were his authentic relationships.

Socially intelligent people understand the importance of honesty, respect, communication, and investment of time in social interactions. On the other hand, those who struggle with making friends often neglect these crucial elements which lead them down a road of loneliness and isolation instead of forming meaningful attachments with others. Let us face it, making friends is not always a walk in the park. Some people seem to effortlessly attract friends while others struggle to expand their social circles, no matter how hard they try. But why is this the case? And how can we navigate the challenges of our increasingly digital and connected world to build deeper, more meaningful relationships?

In a world where people are constantly glued to their smartphones and earbuds, it can be tough to connect and truly engage with those around us. It is a perfect way of saying 'LMAO' without saying the words. But with some simple strategies and a shift in mindset, we can press the refresh button on our interactions and start building the deep, authentic connections we crave. Do not settle for surface-level small talk and emoji-filled texts. Join me and discover the keys to unlocking the power of real human connection.

ENHANCE YOUR SOCIAL SKILLS: 9 STRATEGIES TO THE S.O.C.I.A.L. Y.O.U.

If you want to up your social game, start by having a conversation with yourself - something I like to call 'bathroom talk.' Do you remember Michael Jackson's hit song, 'Man in the Mirror?' It's a hit for a reason - the message is both universal and personal. The lyrics paint a picture of staring at yourself in the mirror and taking responsibility for change.

- **Self-awareness**: To improve your social skills, start by elevating your level of self-awareness. Once you understand your strengths, weaknesses, and triggers in social situations, you can foster open and honest communication by expressing yourself clearly and actively listening to others. Identifying your unique strengths and leading with them can help you in any social interaction. Research has shown that people who have a clear sense of their strengths and values are more likely to achieve their goals. The more you understand and embrace your strengths, the more authentic you can be with others. Once you've identified your strengths and weaknesses, you're ready to tackle the next step.

- **Organization:** Taking the time to organise your thoughts before you speak or interact with others can help you appear more professional, prepared, and help you express yourself clearly. Practice delivering a short speech or presentation, paying attention to your body language, tone of voice, and overall impact. Ask a friend or colleague to provide feedback on how well you captivated and engaged them.

- **Charismatic Communication:** Be relatable and communicate confidently with charisma. Your charisma is a secret weapon for attracting and influencing others. But how do you develop this quality? Start by being authentic and projecting energy. You cannot give from an empty cup. People can tell when you are not being genuine, and this can decrease your likability. Another way to cultivate charisma is by telling great stories. People recall stories more than facts or figures, so it is essential to learn how to tell compelling stories that make you memorable and influential.

- **Improved Intelligence** – You can sharpen both social and emotional intelligence skills by recognising and managing your emotions, understanding the emotions of others, and choosing how you respond versus react. Empathy and emotional regulation can help build better connections with others. Think of a good or bad social experience you have had recently. What made it enjoyable or not so great? Jot down a quick listing of these characteristics, positive and negative, and reflect on them. What can you do better next time?

- **Approachability:** Pay attention to your visuals. This includes, but is not limited to:

  o Appearance/grooming: Yes, no matter what anyone tells you, we still judge a book by its cover. Your appearance says a lot about you and what you care about. Those first few minutes someone spends in your presence can create a lingering first impression that sometimes is hard to forget. I frequently coach my mentees to 'dress for your next level.' What that simply means is to take the extra effort to dress appropriately for the audience, the workplace, or the environment you find yourself in. The way you dress and carry yourself matters. While there is no one 'right' way to dress, it is important to look polished and put together, and to dress appropriately for the occasion. Caveat: You do not have to break the bank to look good.

o Etiquette/poise: How do you show up at work and in life? How organised are you? Do you have a lateness culture, always in a hurry, and focus on yourself and no one else? Do your style and habits reflect your personality and values? How often do you practice active listening during meetings or conversations with others? The quality of your poise and etiquette add up to your executive presence.

- **Listening Actively:** Active listening is one of the simplest but most powerful skills you can develop to become a social superstar. Learn to focus entirely on the speaker and respond thoughtfully to their ideas and feelings. Practice active listening in a conversation with a friend or colleague. Take notes on their interests, concerns, and needs, and follow up with them on those points in a later conversation.

- **Don't be a Yapper**: Have you ever found yourself trapped in a conversation with someone who dominates the discussion and shows little interest in letting you speak your mind? We have all been there. These types of individuals often struggle to be good conversationalists as they tend to interrupt often and cut you off. To be more sociable, learn to create an inclusive environment where everyone's voices are valued.

- **Observe and Improve Your Social Cues:** This includes facial expressions, tone of voice, body language, eye contact, and other gestures. Effective communication is a cornerstone of social competence. It involves both verbal and nonverbal skills. Psychological studies by Albert Mehrabian (1971) emphasise that only 7% of communication relies on words, while 55% is based on body language and 38% on vocal tone. Identify people who appear confident and self-assured socially, observe their demeanour and interactions with others, and mirror some of their techniques (Watch out: Be authentic and congruent with your values).

- **Unstuck Yourself By Developing a Growth Mindset.** It sounds cliché but it is true. Carol Dweck's research showed that there are two different kinds of mindsets - growth and fixed. People with a growth mindset believe that their abilities and intelligence can be developed with hard work, good strategies, and help from others. People with fixed mindsets believe that their abilities and intelligence are set in stone and cannot be changed while growth mindset individuals tend to view setbacks as an opportunity to learn and grow. They persist in the face of difficulties, enjoy challenges, and see effort as the key to success. If you believe you can be more social, you are right. If you believe you can't, you are also right.

STRATEGIES TO DEVELOP YOUR SOCIAL CIRCLE

A few years ago, I was invited to speak to a mentor-mentee group who were meeting physically for the first time in a beautiful garden close to where I lived. I thought about what to share with the group to prepare them for the year-long mentoring relationship journey they were embarking on, and the illustration of the rubber band came to mind. A rubber band has a fundamental purpose - the innate ability to stretch, wrap itself around an object, and hold it in place. A rubber band lying idle on a surface is a waste. Its potential is tested when it is stretched. If you apply tension to a rubber band, it responds by stretching to the challenge, and in the process, it expands.

Approaching new people and groups is like trying to stretch your 'social rubber band' - daunting, but can be worth it. Expanding your social circle demands a desire and corresponding action to move your social status from where you are to where you could be. When opportunities to stretch your social rubber band present themselves, here are some simple baby steps to take that'll make you look like a pro:

- Start with a smile that says, 'I come in peace.' It's a powerful way to create a positive first impression and make others feel at ease.

- Ask questions like you are a curious cat. People love talking about themselves, so give them the chance to do so. Ask open-ended questions that allow for a more extended conversation and prepare to be amazed at what you will learn.

> *If you want to up your social game, start by having a conversation with yourself*

- Find common ground like you are a treasure hunter. Look for shared interests or experiences that you can connect on. It is like finding a goldmine and once you do, conversation flows seamlessly.

- Practice active listening and make them feel heard. It is like giving someone a mental hug. Trust builds and relationships grow as a result. Plus, who doesn't love being heard?

Here is a quick exercise for you that can help you start with who you already have in your circle. Flip through your phone list or professional network and identify ten people you admire. Make a table and reflect on what you like most about them.

Whom I admire	Why I admire them	How can I get to know them better

NAVIGATING DIFFICULT SOCIAL SITUATIONS

Difficult social situations can be challenging to navigate, but it is essential to handle them with grace and poise. We all face disagreements and frustrations sometimes. But what matters most is how we handle them. That is where conflict resolution comes in – the ability to identify the root cause of an issue and work towards a practical solution. Here are some tips for navigating difficult social situations:

- Stay calm: Remaining calm and composed can help to diffuse tension and create a more positive outcome.

- Listen actively: Listen to the other person's perspective and try to understand their point of view. This can help to de-escalate the situation and find a solution that works for everyone.

- Express empathy: Expressing empathy can help to create a sense of understanding and connection. Try to put yourself in the other person's shoes and show that you understand them.

- Set boundaries: If the situation becomes too difficult or uncomfortable, it is important to set boundaries and remove yourself from the situation. This can be done politely and respectfully, but it is essential to prioritise your well-being.

Dr Judith Glaser's research explained that conversations are directly linked to the brain's functionality. The quality of conversations

> **Expanding your social circle demands a desire and corresponding action to move your social status from where you are to where you could be.**

affects the release of certain hormones, such as oxytocin, which are essential in building trust, empathy, loyalty, and other positive emotions. Conversely, negative conversations activate the fight-or-flight response, releasing stress hormones like cortisol, leading to heightened emotions, decreased trust, and an overall negative impact on relationships.

THE SOCIAL YOU AND BLIND SPOTS

What is your blind spot when it comes to building relationships with others? In her book, *Conversational Intelligence*, Dr Judith Glaser highlighted five common blind spots that show up in conversations:

a) Assuming everyone thinks like me: This is the tendency to impose your thoughts and beliefs on others. This blind spot may stop you from considering other perspectives besides your own. Being open-minded and conscious that we all have some form of bias can keep you grounded and agile in thinking.

b) Feelings change our reality: This blind spot appears when we fail to acknowledge that the emotions we feel can sometimes cloud our judgment and ability to deal with reality. Developing emotional intelligence allows us to understand how our feelings impact communication. By doing so, we can relate to others better, leading to more genuine and profound relationships.

c) I am too fearful to empathise: Fear can hold us back from truly connecting with others. With the right mindset, we can cultivate empathy and create meaningful conversations that build trust and understanding.

d) I remember; therefore I know: Our memories can be unreliable, leading to misunderstandings. Dr. Glaser reminds us to approach conversations with an open mind and a willingness to learn. By valuing the perspectives of others, we can broaden our understanding and knowledge.

e) I am listening, so I know what you mean: Active listening is key to effective communication. Dr Glaser shows us that true understanding comes from empathising and seeking clarification. By becoming aware of this blind spot, we can create an environment where individuals feel genuinely heard and understood.

We all have blind spots. When you acknowledge this fact, you raise your level of self-awareness around your listening and speaking and are more open to feedback from others.

SOCIALISING TIPS FOR INTROVERTS

For introverts, socialising with others can sometimes seem intimidating or overwhelming. The thought of stepping out into a crowded networking event and making small talk non-stop is usually not seen as having a great time. Since we have established that social interactions are essential for both personal and professional success, here are some tips to help you connect better with others, even if you prefer solitude:

a) Embrace your introversion: Recognise that networking does not have to involve you being the centre of attention. Focus on building deeper connections with a smaller group of people.

b) Plan ahead: Before attending an event, set an expectation.

Do some research and prepare your mind for what it could entail. What are the possible benefits of attending the event? Identify key people or companies you would like to connect with and come up with thoughtful questions to start a conversation. In some instances, invite a friend along so you have a familiar face around.

c) Start small and challenge yourself the next time: Engage in one-on-ones and grow from there. You may also try smaller events and as you gain more confidence, scale up to bigger events. On virtual platforms, interact in the comment section. Platforms like LinkedIn and Twitter are also good avenues for networking and learning about new opportunities.

d) Practice active listening: As an introvert, this is likely already your superpower. Show you value someone by asking thoughtful questions and listening carefully to their response.

e) Join a network: Joining groups or clubs related to your interests can help you connect with like-minded individuals and build relationships. Being in too many can be overwhelming, so stick to a maximum of three and invest time and attention.

f) Quarterly experiences: Be open to new experiences and opportunities for social connection. Every quarter, plan one thing outside of your comfort zone and give yourself the permission to experience new feelings, gain new insights, and explore the world and people around you better. Each experience does not have to be an expensive venture.

g) Have fun: In as much as it is good to be prepared before an event, balance that with a desire to have fun. Laugh! Mingle! Enjoy the view and the food. Take it all in. Life is meant to be enjoyed. People need hope, humour, and laughter in today's world. Just look around you. It's breaking news every hour. So, be the sunshine! Play to your strengths and do not play small.

SOCIALISING TIPS FOR EXTROVERTS

a) Want to build stronger connections with others? Try listening more and talking less. It may seem counterintuitive, but research shows that active listening skills make you more attractive and trustworthy. Instead of monopolising conversations with your anecdotes or views, ask open-ended questions and give others the space to share their unique perspectives. You will be surprised how much more you can learn and how much deeper your relationships will become.

b) Quality Conversations = Quality Time: Being social is not about winning the title for greeting the highest number of people at the event. Having a quality conversation with a few people far outweighs jumping from one person to another and shoving a business card in their faces. Have you been to a networking event where all people wanted to do was stuff your handbag with their complimentary cards or tell you all about their accolades even before asking for your name? I have and it didn't feel genuine to me. Be sincere in your approach and build trust.

c) Socialise with consideration by picking up on social cues: While you may thrive on socialising, remember that not everyone feels the same way. It's crucial to be perceptive of when someone might be uncomfortable or disinterested and modify your conduct accordingly. This can involve distancing yourself from socialising, giving someone their personal space, and paying attention to their body language.

d) Additionally, repay the favour to your social network: Foster strong relationships based on reciprocity. Although it feels amazing to be supported and aided by others, it is also crucial to give the same support in return. Studies have revealed that by providing help to others, you can increase your pleasure and satisfaction. Overly self-consciousness can throw you off. It's difficult to focus on others or what is going on around you when you are too focused on yourself. It is easy to imagine that people are watching your every move until you know that they are not. We become more alive when we stop focusing on ourselves and start seeing our relationships with one another. When your thoughts are 'How can I assist?' rather than 'I hope they like me,' you turn the attention away from yourself and build more lasting relationships.

e) As an extrovert, it is easy to put on a social mask to make connections but deep and lasting relationships come from being honest and genuine: Research tells us that being open about our thoughts and feelings attracts others to us. So, be your authentic self and share who you are. Remember, building social skills and relationships require intentionality and authenticity. By listening more than you talk, focusing on meaningful connections, paying attention to social cues, contributing to your network, and being true to yourself, you can create strong bonds that will benefit you both personally and professionally.

A man's character may be learned from the adjectives which he habitually uses in conversation - Mark Twain

PERSONAL CHALLENGE

Time to evaluate your current relationships.

- Take a piece of paper, on one side, and list the top five relationships that you have built this year. It may be someone you see every day at home, in the office, in the marketplace, etc. To help you do this quickly, flip through your phone log or social media feeds to see who you have interacted with the most in the last three months.

- On the other side of the paper, I want you to list one word that describes how you feel in that relationship. Picture in your mind meeting with this person and chatting for a few minutes. How do you feel? Happy? Sad? Drained? Excited? Describe it in one word and be honest about it. Did you learn something of value? Did you mentor or give something of value to this person? Has the relationship transformed your life positively?

- Check-in with your feelings at this very moment and what you have written down. Which relationship do you want to strengthen, start, or stop?

In summary, social interactions can be intimidating, especially for those who struggle with social anxiety or find it challenging to navigate new situations. However, building strong relationships is essential for personal and professional success. Whether you are looking to expand your social circle, develop new business connections, or improve your dating life, I hope these tips and strategies help you thrive in any social setting.

It always seems impossible until someone becomes unstoppable. Let that someone be YOU. Be unstoppable!

CHAPTER 7

THE NEUROSCIENCE OF CHANGE

By Niyi Borire

Change is inevitable. Change is a force that cannot be stopped or curtailed. Change is a natural phenomenon - this is a foundational statement. We all are in a constant state of change. Our bodies, brains and minds are in continually changing. Change can sometimes happen to us when we do not expect it. This often comes along in the form of a disruption. Everything gets disrupted, and the whole dynamic is altered.

Recently, we had federal elections in Australia, and our Prime Minister was voted out of office. This was one of the most significant shifts in the political landscape of Australia. This man won in a landslide three years ago, but the people voted him out at the next election. Even though he successfully navigated the nation through the COVID-19 pandemic, the goodwill he enjoyed had expired, and the masses had turned on him. The alternative political party had won, not by increasing their voter share, but because the Prime Minister lost his base, who had moved to the independent candidates. These independents were not aligned with any party, but they disrupted the system by taking away the voters of the major parties.

Sometimes, change comes into our lives when we are unprepared for it. It comes into our lives and hits us like a massive wave. A lot of people struggle to adapt to change, and a lot of people struggle to react to change in a prompt manner or in a way that will help them keep their purpose and maintain their focus. When I started this journey of reaching out and helping people, my purpose was clear to me. My vision was to help people navigate change without losing their purpose, identity, or individuality.

What often happens is that when change occurs to you, wildly when unexpected, you are likely to compromise your values. You might feel like deviating from your purpose. Some time ago, I was teaching my inner circle about the differences between distractions and detours. Whilst distractions take us away from the path to our destiny, detours slow our journeys allowing us time to prepare ourselves for our assignments. When change happens, there is a tendency to walk away from your original plan and from your purpose, and if you are not careful, you would lose your identity and individuality. The challenge, then, is how can we successfully navigate change without losing who we are and what we stand for. How can you remain on your path or stay aligned with your journey when disruption occurs? This is what a lot of people struggle with.

YOU CAN CREATE YOUR CHANGE

The interesting aspect of this discourse is that we can create the change we desire. A lot of people are satisfied with reacting to change. They are reactionary, not visionary, They are not prepared for change, so when it comes, they struggle to adapt and they crumble. There is another level you can operate from – creating your desired change. This is certainly possible, but potentially difficult if you are not well informed. Why do some people struggle to create change in their lives, families, lifestyles, businesses, or health. Some are able to initiate the process of change, but they struggle to sustain it. The reason why many start creating change but are unable to complete it is not due to the lack of purpose or resources. It is due to a lack of knowledge about the principles that govern change. This is what I will be sharing briefly – the Neuroscience of Change.

> **When change happens, there is a tendency to walk away from your original plan and from your purpose, and if you are not careful, you would lose your identity and individuality.**

I will approach change creation from a neuroscientific point of view and explore the reasons why it is difficult to create sustainable change. Why do you struggle to create new habits, particularly in the area of personal performance? A lot of us struggle, we know exactly what to do, and we know the areas of our lives that need improvement, but identification without execution will not change anything. Even when you get paid coaches, mentors, or attend conferences, you still struggle to execute them. No programme or online conference will exert the transformative influence that you require if you do not understand the basis of change. If you do not understand how the brain works when it comes to change, no number of conferences or books will make a difference. Change has to begin with you and it starts with your understanding. You are reading this book because you want to move from where you are to where you want to be. This movement is very difficult for some people, particularly in terms of their performance.

I am not going to be addressing organisational change or change in your relationships. I am going to focus on personal transformation and self-development. If you take a detailed look at yourself, I am sure you'll find some habits you want to change. Habits are hard to change because habits have three foundational components. Every habit has (1) an observable behaviour, as well as underlying (2) emotions and (3) thought patterns.

There is usually an emotional component to every habit that you have. Let us take the habit of overthinking as a case study. If you overthink or overanalyse issues, at the foundation of that habit is an emotional undertone. Emotions are natural biological programmes and processes that occur in our minds in reaction to certain situations. When you encounter a situation, at the subconscious level you generate an emotion.

Every individual generates about 150 emotions every hour and most of those emotions are non-conscious. It takes about 8 milliseconds from the time that your emotion is generated to the time that you are fully conscious of the emotion. Although you may be unaware of these emotions, they are still present – operating like background music. They dictate your inner atmosphere. They prime you for action, dictating the tune of your behavioural responses and reactions.

Habits are formed in response to emotional triggers. A habit is a response to a trigger, or a cue. The habit of overthinking has to be triggered. The cue could be a pending decision or quick choice. Maybe you are at the shop and you have got two items to choose from. Or you encounter a T-junction while driving, and you're struggling to decide which way to turn. Every time you are given a choice to make, the habit is triggered. What you may not realise is that this situation also generates an emotion within you. The emotion could be fear, anxiety or curiosity. Whatever it is, it looks like it is unpleasant. You may not be able to describe it as fear, maybe you are not threatened but that emotion is there and that emotion creates the foundation for overthinking.

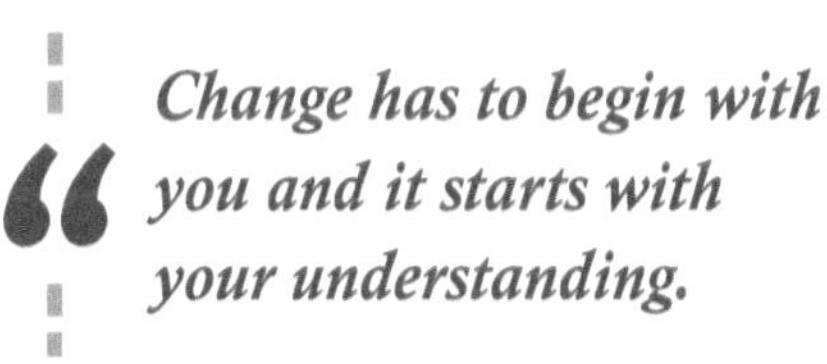

Let us take procrastination as another example. Let us say you have a task to submit a paper. That is the trigger, that is the cue. The natural response for you should be getting it done as soon as possible, but your underlying emotions and thoughts kick in. When you get a reminder to do a task, the emotional response generated in you is frustration, tiredness, or fear. They are all negative emotions and you may not be able

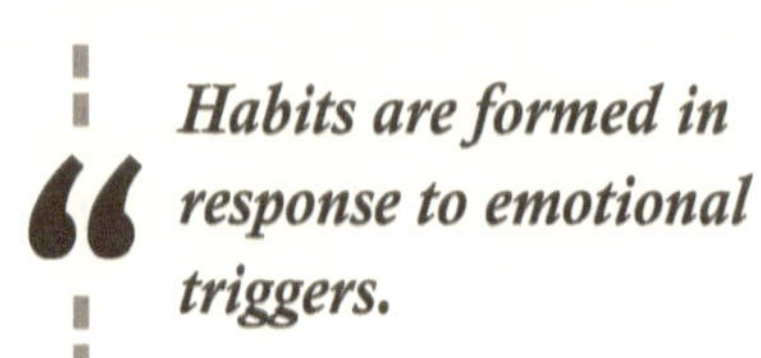

to characterise them that way. You may not get typical physiological responses, like racing heartbeat and sweaty palms, but it is still an unpleasant experience. You may not be fully conscious of it, but there is an emotional component to procrastination. This creates a foundation for the next aspect of your habit which is your thought pattern. Every habit has a thinking component, which comes before the behaviour is carried out. People procrastinate, but they don't understand that there is a self-defeating thought pattern that underlies their procrastination. If you are going to fix a habit, you have to fix the thought patterns that underlie it.

THE SCIENCE OF HABITS

So, for the person who procrastinates, the trigger is 'do something.' There is an emotional response that you cannot control. Those emotions are there, they are usually brief, and maybe in your situation, those emotions translate into feelings that are much longer. You feel discouraged about the task — it would seem too difficult to do. You feel afraid that this is going to take up all your time. You are not just procrastinating because you are lazy or uncommitted to the course, you are not procrastinating because you don't care, you probably care enough for you to identify that you have got a problem with procrastination, but the issue is that there are some emotional undertones that you need to be aware of.

On top of that is the thinking pattern. You start thinking about the emotions you feel. So, it starts with a feeling. Every habit starts with a feeling then thinking and then behaving.

Feeling > Thinking > Doing.

Beneath the habit, there is a feeling, which is then followed by thinking before doing. For someone who procrastinates, the feelings can be overwhelming because they are already hardwired. They then develop negative thoughts which reinforce the emotional undertone, thus priming them for action. This process makes it extremely difficult to break the habit of procrastination, because the individual is already primed at the emotional and cognitive level.

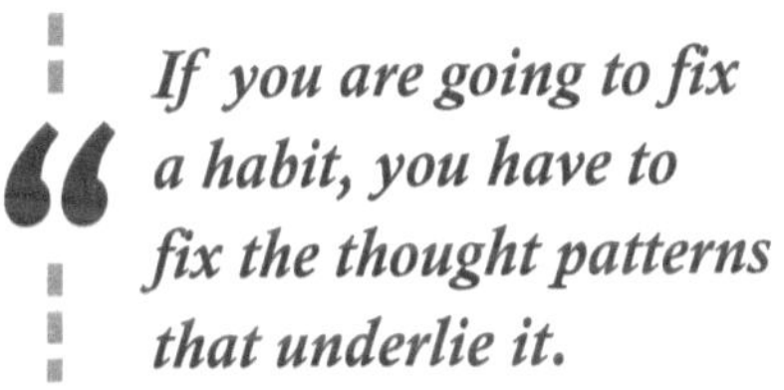

For instance, the moment you see a red traffic light while driving, your legs are already positioned on the brakes - you are primed for action. Your car may not be moving, but your engine is revving. That is what your emotions do to you. When the trigger comes, your engine is revved up for action. You know you are going to commit the habit once you're exposed to the cue. It might be something you are ashamed of, like masturbation, pornography, etc. Every time you get the trigger, you get primed and aroused at the emotional level. What next? You start thinking about it. That is where the issue is. Your thought patterns can reinforce the feelings. '*I am feeling this way*', '*I don't think I can do this*', '*Oh! I am confused.*' So, if the thought pattern is haphazard and self-defeating, for a person who overanalyses, they just repeat the same thing over and over again. Of course, you will be more confused and those thoughts will make the feelings of anxiety and all other negative feelings more prominent. What happens at the end of the day? You just feel frustrated, and you drop your work. You end up in a fix and start panicking. Maybe if you have learnt how to control your feelings, you will be able to see clearly and make the choice - maybe the right choice is even there.

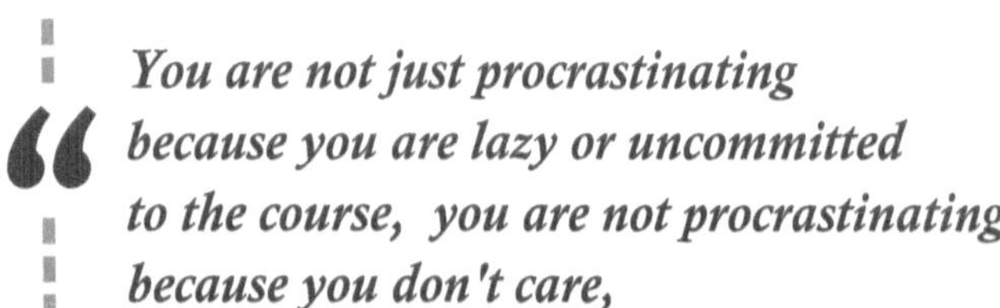

> **You are not just procrastinating because you are lazy or uncommitted to the course, you are not procrastinating because you don't care,**

For the person who overanalyses, how many times have you asked someone else 'A or B' and they are like what are you talking about? You know it is A. The correct choice was A all along, but because you were faced with that choice and some of those neural circuits in your brain have been formed to generate these emotional responses, every time that trigger comes, the feeling you get is of emotional exasperation; a feeling of frustration, a feeling of anger, a feeling that you are overwhelmed and you think about it more. The more you think about it, you end up repeating it and you get more and more overwhelmed. What happens? You end up not making a decision. If it is procrastination, the same thing goes. You feel overwhelmed and you let go of the task you have. You push it away and you move on. That is how habits are formed.

I have just broken down to you what habits are and how difficult it will be for people to break habits. Many people think that habits are about what they do. No! Your habits are not in your doing. Your habits are in your feeling, thinking, and then doing. Everything that you do repetitively has an emotional, thinking, and behavioural component to it. So, when people say old habits die hard, there is a reason why that is the case. It is because all of these three different components of habits are hardwired in your brain.

THE NEUROSCIENCE OF HABITS

There is a certain law in neuroscience, *the Hebb's Law*, which states that old neuronal circuits are not deconstructed. What that means is that every habit has neuronal circuits within your brain. The brain is composed of nerve cells called neurons. Nerves communicate with each other at junctions, called synapses. There are neural-networks in your brain that have been built by your habits. Every time this neural circuit is triggered, the outcome is that there is a desire to perform the habit. Usually, there is always a trigger for every habit. Every time that trigger occurs, the response is a desire for the habit. It starts with the feeling, moves to the thinking, and then ends with the doing. It starts at the subconscious level even before you act on it. Once that trigger is activated, the feeling is activated. Emotions are subconscious. Once they get to the cortex of the brain, you start to feel them and you start thinking about the satisfaction you will get from the habit.

The feeling part of the brain called the limbic system is where your emotions are generated. The thinking part of the brain called the prefrontal cortex is part of the brain that controls your inhibition. Every time you feel like doing something, your thinking part of the brain (the prefrontal cortex) will analyse that feeling to see whether it is appropriate. Imagine you are driving your car and someone hits you. You step out of the car rehearsing in your head what you would say to the person, '*I am going to deal with you today. Why did you hit my car? Why are you driving rough?*' Then you get to the culprit's car only to find a giant. You find somebody a 6 feet 9 inches muscular giant. Very quickly, your anger would disappear without any thought because you know that person can deal with you. That is your thinking brain. That is your prefrontal cortex telling you to calm down even though you are angry.

That is why you can remain calm when you are annoyed by your boss. You suck it in. You do not talk, even though on the inside you are boiling and you feel like dealing with your boss. You suck it up because you know that he pays your salary. But of course, if the person giving you a hard time is a subordinate, you will let them know. You will tongue-lash them and you will express your anger and do all of that. Why are you able to vary your behaviour when you have the same feelings and the same triggers? It is the same feeling of anger you feel because someone smashed your car but you behave differently depending on whether the person can deal with you or the person cannot. That is the thinking part of the brain at work. So, what happened between the time you stepped out of your car because someone hit it and when you finally got to the person? While you are taking that action of stepping out of your car, your prefrontal cortex is analysing the situation and immediately you see someone who can beat you up, you quickly simmer. You smile and try to handle it nicely. But if it was someone else, you may raise your voice because of your prefrontal cortex.

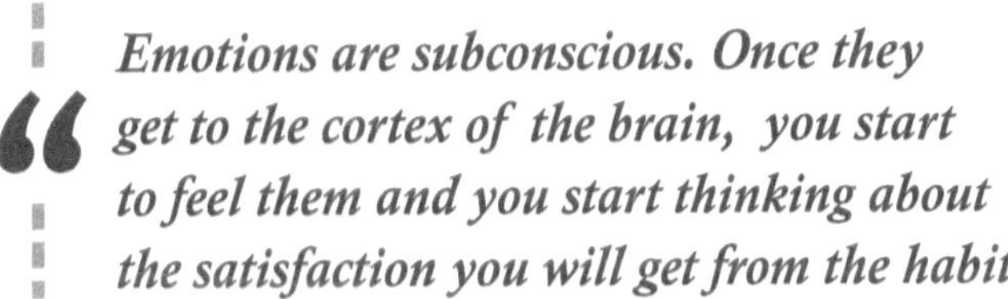

> *Emotions are subconscious. Once they get to the cortex of the brain, you start to feel them and you start thinking about the satisfaction you will get from the habit.*

Pretty much, I am just using this example to illustrate the point to you that every habit has underlying emotions and thinking patterns. Most people do not know that the efficiency and productivity of your brain depend on the time of the day. Some people have morning brains – meaning their brains operate at peak performance in the morning. Others have afternoon brains, and some others have evening brains.

Most people are not aware of this fact, so they struggle a lot. You will never be as productive as you should be. Maybe it is time to look into some of these things.

We have established that habits have three components to them – we have the emotional component, the thinking component, and the behaviour component. A lot of us focus on the behaviour not realising that you cannot just switch off a habit if you don't deal with the feeling and the thinking. Remember that the feeling and the thinking that underlies the doing of every habit are already hardwired. There are already circuits that are activated with every performance of a habit. Every habit has a trigger and that trigger creates a response of a feeling, the feeling leads to thinking, and you end up doing it. It is quite difficult for people to change their habits because of this reason. When people say old habits die hard, it is because of the existing wiring in your brain. Anything that is hardwired in your brain does not deconstruct. How do you deal with this? It is by forming new connections. If your trigger is chilli, for instance, you cannot break it down. You have to form a new circuit that will be connected to chilli and maybe it will be drinking water. That neuronal circuit that underpins the habit you want to change is not going to get destroyed. The emotional feelings will still be there, and the emotional cravings will still be there. They won't go and of course, when you do not use something over some time, you lose it.

If there are neurons in your brain that you are not activating, over time they stop firing. They do not go away but they stop firing. That is why drug addicts go into detox to overcome their cravings. But if you give a drug addict a drug twenty years after they have been clean, those emotional responses will be resurrected. That is why drug addicts can relapse at any time because the existing wiring does not break down. The wiring of your brain that encodes the emotional responses of your habits does not break down. They will not go away even with prayer and fasting. I am a person of faith, but I am talking about science here and how we can use our knowledge of science to better our lives and our habits. Please, get it straight that those existing wiring will not go away. Your goal now will be to form new habits.

You may not be able to stop the feeling of a habit, but you have got to deal with your thinking because your thinking is the bridge from your feeling to your doing. The area of intervention will be in your thinking patterns. By working on your thinking patterns, you will be able to modulate your feelings over time. We do that by forming new networks over time. That takes time. It takes you identifying your goal and focusing your attention on that habit. This involves coaching, support, and mentoring - somebody holding you accountable. It takes a lot of work, but you can go through that change that you require. Once you understand the basis of this, you have to start with '*Why am I feeling the way I am feeling?*' '*Why am I thinking the way I think?*' '*What are my thought patterns?*' You have got to reflect and interface yourself. Sometimes, you may need somebody to hold your hand and walk through that journey with you. But that is something that you must commit yourself to. As you do that, you will find out that you can build new habits.

THE CHANGE CURVE

Every new habit goes through a change curve. Initially, when you identify what you want to do, the first thing that occurs is a period of excitement and anticipation. At that time, your expectations are high, and you are pumped up. Maybe you have just attended a masterclass on reading, you heard a speaker talk about reading and you are so pumped up and excited about it. You may find yourself on Amazon buying books. You may buy five to ten books. Maybe you watched a webinar by your mentor talking about the books they have read and you just go online on a spending spree and you are excited. On the first day, you open the first book and read chapters 1, 2, and 3. With time, what happens is that other competitive activities for your attention come along. You have not taken time to look at the feeling, and the thinking before doing. You just moved to the doing. You did not take time to think about why you want to be a reader, what is your goal? Are you just reading because you want to get something?

Let me use myself as an example when it comes to reading. A lot of the time, I do not finish a book. I am not a fan of '*I have read 10 books this year*' For what? I read based on my season. There are a lot of books that I have only read a chapter because that was what spoke to me at that time. That is it for me. I understand my why. That why is what sets the tone for your thinking and your feelings. Perhaps your thinking is *'Because this person reads 10 books, I have to be a reader,'* or *'I have to finish the Bible.'* It is good to read the Bible from cover to cover, but what is your reason? Is it so that you can come out and say you have read the Bible 30 times? I would prefer to get stuck on one verse of the Bible for one month, full of revelation and growth, than to read the whole Bible in a year and most of it does not speak to me or I cannot remember anything from it.

Every time you want to start a new habit, you are excited, there is an anticipation but that anticipation is quickly replaced by anxiety, frustration, and despair because the initial arousal stress has been lost. Your initial arousal stress is not sustainable. Those initial feelings dissipate because those feelings are not deep. The foundation of the feeling is based on the *what*, not the *why*. If you want to form a new habit, you have got to start with the *WHY*. If you have read Simon Sinek's book, *Start With Why*, he mentioned that a lot of people start with the what - what I want to do. They do not start with the *why*. Why do you want to learn this new musical instrument? Why do you want to take that course? Why do you want to start the business? What is your *why*? Your *what* may be fancy and fashionable, but you have to start with the *why*.

The change curve is that there is an initial period of excitement and anticipation that is quickly replaced by anxiety and resistance to change. You just have to go back to your old ways. You see your books and you feel bad about not reading much. You do not want to buy any more books. You just feel dispelled and all that. That is a natural phase and of course, if you put the right strategies in place, you can build that excitement again. However, what will help sustain that will be your why, accountability, creativity, and how you can make some lifestyle choices that will help sustain that change.

CHAPTER 8

CONCLUSION: THE WHOLE YOU

Imagine that you have a car and just because you love the interior so much, that is all you ever concentrate on about the car. You read up on ways in which you can make the interior better always and you ensure you apply whatever methods you discover from your reading. You do not bother about the other parts because they do not interest you like the car interior. Would that not be strange? Ignoring every other part of the car just because you are naturally attracted to one part is a disaster waiting to happen. If you do not pay attention to other things such as checking the oil levels, water level, gauging the tyres, etc., it is only a matter of time before the car breaks down and it will not matter how nice the interior looks. The car must be taken care of as a whole.

We hope it has been a great journey so far reading about what it takes to change you. The idea was not just to bombard you with information or make you feel bad about areas where you have seen the need to change. Our aim for writing is to empower you to change the *whole you*. Yes, the *whole you*. While you may be tempted to focus on the areas of change that resonate the most with you, the truth is that every area of life that we have addressed is important. None is more important than the other. You cannot say you are just interested in the interior (say the spiritual you) and you leave out all other aspects. The *whole you* comprises of these different parts. As a result, changing you requires changing the *whole you* - the creative you, the spiritual you, the emotional you, the financial you, the physical you, and the social you. It is a complete package.

Just like the car, which will only function well when all its parts are well taken care of, the *whole you* must be paid attention to and challenged to change. It is possible to give the attention that each part of *you* needs to become better. That is why we have provided this toolkit which you can always refer to in order to ensure your ongoing all-round transformation. Remember that no aspect of *you* is less important than the other. In fact, it is God's desire that you prosper in your spirit, soul, and body. So, that should be your goal too. It is the reason why we wrote this book.

Remember that change is a process, so you do not need to be too hard on yourself. We encourage you to highlight areas where you need to change and the specific steps you need to take to achieve that. Getting an accountability partner that would ensure you follow through will not be a bad idea. We strongly recommend it.

It is one chance we all have to live life to the fullest on this side of eternity, so we must make it count. You know what you need to do now to become a better you, and by extension, create a better society for all, so go ahead and do it. It may be difficult at first, but you will finally master the process and become the champion of your change. The goal is to change the *whole you*, so go for it. Be all that you can be and do all that you can do. We are rooting for you, and we await your 'changing you' testimonies. See you on the other side - the better side of *you*. Cheers.

References

[i] Genesis 1:1

[ii] Psalm 19:1-4

[iii] Genesis 11:1-9

[iv] Genesis 11:6 NLT

[v] Genesis 2:7 NLT

[vi] Job 32:8 NLT

[vii] Romans 12:6-8

[viii] A copy of the first impression of the Beehive concept on paper

[ix] Source: https://www.td.org/insights/the-neuroscience-of-reward-and-threat

[x] https://www.eurosport.com/football/premier-league/2015-2016/leicester-city-s-premier-league-title-win-the-greatest-underdog-story-of-all_sto5521114/story.shtml

[xi] Genesis 1:26 NLT

[xii] Genesis 2:7 NIV

[xiii] https://holdingtotruth.com/2013/07/21/what-is-the-function-of-your-spirit/

[xiv] 1 John 1:3 NLT

[xv] John 4:24 NLT

[xvi] 1 Corinthians 2:11 GNT

[xvii] Job 32:8 NLT

[xviii] https://en.m.wikipedia.org/wiki/Spiritual_intelligence#:~:text=Operationalizing%20the%20construct%2C%20they%20defined,and%20commitment%20to%20human%20values.%22

xix Matthew 14:14-21 NLT

xx Luke 6:36 NLT

xxi Colossians 3:12 NIV

xxii Genesis 1:26-28 NLT

xxiii Isaiah 1:19 NET

xxiv Proverbs 10:28 NLT

xxv Genesis 11:6 KJV

xxvi 2 Timothy 1:7 NLT

xxvii Job 32:8 NIV

xxviii Daniel 5:12 NLV

xxix Colossians 3:13 ESV

xxx 2 Corinthians 4:16 NLT

xxxi Proverbs 18:14 CEB

xxxii Romans 8:28 NLT

xxxiii 2 Corinthians 8:21 NLT

xxxiv 1 Peter 2:2

xxxv 2 Timothy 2:7 NIV

xxxvi Hebrews 11:3 NIV

xxxvii https://konmari.com/about-the-konmari-method/.

xxxviii Proverbs 23:7

xxxix WeMoney, Financial Wellness Survey 2 021- 2022 (2022) p 4.

xl https://www.aihw.gov.au/reports/chronic -disease/chronic-condition-multimorbidity/contents/chronic-conditions-and-multimorbidity

xli BreastCancer.org

xlii https://www.cdc.gov/physicalactivity/basics/pa-health/index.htm

xliii daily consumption of even one hot dog

xliv https://facty.com/conditions/cancer/foods-that-could-cause-cancer/2/

xlv https://www.google.com/search?q=effects+of+nutricion+in+body&rlz=1C1CHBD_en-GBAU920AU920&oq=effects+of+nutricion+in+body&aqs=chrome..69i57j33i10i22i29i30l2.12403j0j15&sourceid=chrome&ie=UTF-8

xlvi https://facty.com/conditions/cancer/foods-that-could-cause-cancer/11/

xlvii https://lovelifebefit.com/how-running-changes-your-body/,

xlviii https://ods.od.nih.gov/factsheets/VitaminD-HealthProfessional/

xlix https://myhealth.alberta.ca/Alberta/Pages/Setting-smart-goals.aspx

NIYI BORIRE

Niyi Borire is an award-winning neurologist, researcher and NeuroLeadership expert. He is a thought leader and founder of Legacy Consults, a leadership development outfit.Niyi is also an Amazon-bestselling author, pastor, executive coach, university lecturer, entrepreneur and a senior officer in the Royal Australian Airforce. He is married to Yemi and they are blessed with two boys.

MOFOLUWASO ILEVBARE

Dr. Mofoluwaso Ilevbare is a multi award-winning HR Thought Leader, Transformational Speaker, and Coach, passionate about leadership development and helping others be unstoppable at work and in life. Fofo, as she is fondly called, lives in Sydney Australia with her family, and has a healthy appetite for chocolate cake.

CHARLES BALL

Charles Ball is a Youth Pastor and language researcher with a passion for relational ministry and counselling. He lives in Sydney, Australia with his family and enjoys spending time with his amazing wife and son.

SAMUEL EKUNDAYO

Dr Samuel Ekundayo is an Harvard-trained transformational speaker, distinguished Senior Lecturer, author and life coach. Often referred to as 'The Purpose Preacher', his calling is to help individuals discover their purpose and maximise their potential. He is the visionary behind the School of Purpose and Influence (SPIN), an esteemed institution dedicated to nurturing individuals for trans-generational influence and global impact. He is married to a woman he calls his Treasure – Dr Blessing Ekundayo - and they are blessed with two boys.

Meet the Authors

ESTHER ADEYINKA

Esther Adeyinka is a lawyer, business owner, advocate and advisory board member. Esther is particularly interested in advocating for and with young people, especially in spaces where their voices aren't often heard. Esther is currently based in Sydney, Australia. She enjoys spending her free time in the sun with a good book or with friends.

TOLU OLIAKU

Tolu Oliaku, a Business Development Manager and Therapeutic Carer, provides mentorship and leadership with a positive outlook. She is dedicated to unleashing potential through practical insights. In addition to her professional achievements, Tolu is an emerging author and a former athlete who earned a Basketball scholarship at the age of 15. Currently residing in Sydney, she enjoys exploring her newfound passions for food, language, and travel.